The Safety Effect

David Moerlein

Published by Moerlein Publishing LLC, Cincinnati, OH, USA,
45242

Figure 15 on page 182 adapted with the permission of the
Intercultural Development Inventory.

ISBN: 979-8-218-33904-3

DEDICATION

I dedicate this book to my family. You encourage and inspire me.

CONTENTS

Introduction 1

**Part One: Understand the Benefits of Psychological
Safety for Business and You** 7

1: Humans Want to Feel Safe 13

2: You Matter 29

3: Invite, Share, and Listen 37

**Part Two: Personal Journey—Establish the Basis for
Psychological Safety** 45

4: Be Patient. Growth Is Difficult. 51

5: Embrace the Learning Journey 63

**Part Three: Team Integration—Support Psychological
Safety Within the Team** 81

6: Share Stories 85

7: Set Goals Aligned to Purpose 109

8: Support the Path Forward 123

9: Partner for Success 141

**Part Four: Cultural Impact—Influence Psychological
Safety Across Your Organization** 163

10: Give a Voice to All 169

11: Embrace Differences 179

Part Five: Build the Habit of Psychological Safety.............187

12: Practice Deliberately....................................189

13: Pursue Flow 201

Conclusion...209

Afterword: Psychological Safety When It's Needed Most 213

Acknowledgments 217

About the Author...221

Notes 223

INTRODUCTION

This is a book for those of us who want to be successful in our careers while doing great things for the world. It will give you tools to support exceptional business outcomes while building happiness for yourself and those around you.

The journey that led to my writing *The Safety Effect* began almost four decades ago. My memory of that time is filled with emotion and light on details. I was still younger than ten years old, but I had reached an age when I could comfortably set small goals for myself and was beginning to build a sense of what I cared about most. Like now, my family was one of the most important things in my life. So, I wanted to give my mom a gift that would let her know how much she meant to me.

I worked to get enough money, walked into a store and bought what I felt was the perfect gift. I handed it to my mom and said, "This is what I want to do when I grow up." She slowly opened the box and from it lifted a five-inch statue. In her hand, she held a likeness of a boy holding a stethoscope up to a globe.

Little did I know that gift would set the stage for much of the rest of my life.

I felt at a young age that I wanted to do good for the world. Perhaps seemingly contradictory outside of a few careers, I also felt I wanted to make a lot of money. That special gift, after all, wasn't free of charge.

These feelings stuck with me as I grew older, and they often felt at odds with each other. From what I could see, people doing good in the world often lacked the wealth I hoped to achieve. The wealthy often did not approach business in a way that served the greater good. I struggled to find a model to obtain both.

When I went to college, I tried again to find a way to merge my goals. After attending three undergraduate institutions, dropping out briefly and changing majors from Chemistry to Biology, I finally graduated with an Ecology degree. I followed that with a Master of Biology, where I studied the ability of plants to remove pollutants from indoor air and improve human health. Mine was the only study at the time to build on the findings of Dr. Wolverton at NASA[1].

With my understanding of how humans, plants, and animals work together I thought I could find a financially viable connection between all of them. I thought I could find a job where I could do good and make a lot of money. But I was wrong.

After more than twenty failed job applications, I once again reassessed my approach. This time, I pursued a degree I expected would be more conducive to finding a job—an MBA at The University of Michigan. But I never felt fully at ease there. Perhaps this was because it was my first experience with a group of people, many of them great individuals, who were very focused on money and profits. This is a big shift from the world of Biology, where people will dedicate a lifetime to studying spider dancing and mating rituals, with little interest in money.

I shifted from a world focused on the attainment of knowledge, sometimes in the absence of an immediate external reward, to a world focused on profit.

Then I found Google.

No company is perfect, but Google was exactly what I had been looking for since I gave that statue to my mom. It makes a lot of money, with a $1.6 trillion market cap[2] and nearly $300 billion in annual revenue[3] at the time of writing. Google also does great things for the world. The company provides many free products[4], empowers nonprofit organizations through Google.org, provides substantial annual global relief aid, is one of the largest alternative energy investors in the world, and achieved carbon neutrality in 2010[5]. In my experience leading Google Ad sales teams, I also saw the direct benefit of Google for our advertising customers and their customers.

I finally found a workplace where I could do good for the world while making money, and I spent the next 15 years of my professional life there.

During my time at Google, I managed 145 people across ten global offices within the Global Business Organization including sales, customer service, and enablement. I also brought my approach to the Google.org Fellowship, where I worked as part of a team of pro bono software engineers, product managers, and UX designers and researchers to support access to government assistance. My teams worked with thousands of Google Ads customers, launched Google's first seller skills training to our SMB sales organization, won a Brandon Hall Award for a project we co-led in support of Google's managers, and consistently exceeded enablement benchmarks for global training.

We drove this success while sustaining a great team culture, strong operations, and individual happiness. My teams expressed their satisfaction in Google's annual manager feedback surveys, where they rated me on average eleven percentage points better than other managers in the Global Business Organization and voted for me to receive numerous excellence awards.

Perhaps most importantly, they also provided candid unsolicited comments. Some comments were very complimentary; they appreciated that I created space for everyone to communicate and share feedback and ideas to improve, without fear. They also shared direct feedback for me to improve. They knew I wanted to serve them well, and they were comfortable sharing how I could do better. Their comfort expressed within these comments was essential to our success.

Several years into my career, I attended a Google training and learned that what I was replicating across teams was called *psychological safety*. For me and many of my teams, that magic enabled us to do great things for ourselves and the world while pursuing record profits.

Scientists have explored the human need to feel emotionally safe for centuries, but it apparently wasn't until the 1960s when Edgar Schein and Warren Bennis referred to this need as *psychological safety*[6]. Since then, several academic and business thought leaders have continued to explore *psychological safety*, notably Harvard's Amy Edmondson. Dr. Edmondson describes *psychological safety* as "a belief that one will not be punished or humiliated for speaking up with ideas, questions, concerns, or mistakes, and that the team is safe for interpersonal risk-taking[7]." Through her decades of research, Edmondson has found significant evidence that personal and business benefits increase when we have high psychological safety. For those rare companies and teams that can create it, the results are overwhelmingly positive for the individuals and business.

In 2012, Google reinforced Edmondson's findings in Project

Aristotle[8]. The company conducted a study across 180 engineering and sales teams, including high and low performers. They controlled variables for key demographic data, hoping to identify what team composition would drive the most effective teams. After analyzing multiple data sets across 35 statistical models and hundreds of variables, they found an unexpected result.

Psychological safety is the number one driver of team effectiveness.

In this study the collocation of teammates, consensus driven decision-making, individual team performance, seniority, team size, and tenure had no significant connection to team effectiveness. The results were clear and have been reinforced by others, across industries. It is psychological safety that supports the creation of high functioning teams that drive business results.

Each of us experiences psychological safety differently. Our comfort with sharing ideas is influenced by multiple factors: our previous experiences, status within our company, social norms, race, gender identification, and many other things. As a result, there is no one approach to build psychological safety within a company. It can vary across teams. One size does not fit all.

Recognizing this variability, I've spent more than a decade reading books and academic and popular articles to build a cross-discipline understanding of how we create safe spaces. I've combined my experience with experts from across psychology, behavioral economics, business acumen, statistics, operations, and others to try to find the approaches that most consistently provide positive feelings of psychological safety.

This book does not provide a how-to guide for building psychological safety. Instead, it will provide you an understanding of the value of psychological safety, along with tools for you and your teams to consider using. I invite you to select the tools that feel most genuine to you, and perhaps ignore the others for now. You will see opportunities to build psychological safety for yourself, your team, and your organization.

Decades of research support what I've strived to achieve most of my life. The advancement of psychological safety has the ability to help you improve the world around you, creating happier teams, improving team performance, and driving business results. There is no foolproof way to build psychological safety, but the following pages will share what I've learned, so you can arrive at success more quickly than I did.

I hope you enjoy the journey!

PART ONE:

Understand the Benefits of Psychological Safety for Business and You

Researchers, academics and industry experts have studied psychological safety for decades. They have shared their findings and expertise in books and articles, each reinforcing the other about how psychologically safe organizations are more likely to retain happy and engaged employees and more quickly identify ways to improve. As a result, these organizations often outperform their peers.

These experts also offer very helpful ideas for how to support the development of psychological safety in the organizations where we work. Dr. Amy Edmondson shares a Leader's Tool Kit to help leaders set the stage for safety, invite participation, and respond productively[9]. Several leadership consultants have also provided their own approaches. The co-founders of the Academy of Brain-based Leadership frame psychological safety in terms of our feelings of security, autonomy, fairness, esteem, trust, and you, appropriately summarized as The S.A.F.E.T.Y. Model[10]. The founder of LeaderFactor considers our psychological safety across multiple levels - inclusion, learner, contributor, and challenger safety[11]. Karolin Helbig and Minette Norman provide several ways to practice building psychological safety within your team[12].

Each of these is a great resource to support your and your team's integration of psychological safety, and I encourage you to check them out. But each left me craving more.

If psychologically safe organizations can support a magical nirvana of employee happiness and motivation aligned to improved business performance, and if experts have been sharing how to create it for decades, why has every company not yet created this safety for their employees? There must be a gap between the understanding of benefits and the activation in the workplace!

Based on my 12 years of leading teams at Google and decades of reviewing theories of human behavior, I've identified three significant factors that hold us back from creating psychological safety at work. The first is the challenge each of us faces when we learn something new, particularly when we are asked to be vulnerable, as this can make us feel very uncomfortable at work. The second is the apparent disconnect between the soft skills of psychology and the perpetual short-term goals required to succeed in our jobs. The third is related to the difficulty of making changes across an organization that already has existing norms and expectations. Changing a company culture can feel overwhelming.

During my last four years at Google, my teams and I developed training for thousands of Googlers across sales, enablement, data analysts, operations, and leadership. During that time, I led hundreds of meetings with Googlers to understand their needs and how we could best support them. These meetings were sometimes with people newer to their careers, but more often with tenured leaders who could oversee teams of hundreds of Googlers.

The lesson from these conversations was largely consistent. Most of them had little interest in taking time away from their workday to pursue training on what they considered soft skills, especially if the training required them to feel vulnerable in front of their peers and leadership. Even if they expressed high interest, the soft skill training would regularly be delayed or abandoned in favor of achieving a short-term business goal. It is easier to default to our existing habits, especially when those habits have helped us achieve our goals in the past, than to pursue something new. This is true, even if the new skill can help us and those around us achieve even greater success.

Sales teams were most interested in how to make the call, lead the meeting, and close the deal. Enablement teams wanted to develop the best training that would share the right information, inspire practice of a new skill, and drive behavior change across the target audience. Operations teams wanted to learn how to project plan, influence without authority, and complete the initiatives for which they were tasked. Leadership often wanted to simultaneously support the well-being of their teams while achieving their short and long-term goals.

When overwhelmed with other work demands, learning how to implement things like psychological safety often was perpetually delayed.

My goal is to build on the great work of others and address the challenges that hold us back from making difficult changes to our behavior. I hope to inspire more organizations to integrate psychological safety now, no longer delaying it for the future. To achieve this, I will help each of us reflect on the challenges and fears we might face, as we learn this new skill of building psychological safety. Through this, we can begin to embrace vulnerability at work. I will help us make a more direct connection between the so-called soft skill of building psychological safety and our team's business operations. And I will support new thinking about how we can have a broader impact across the organizations in which we work. We will then culminate in a reflection about how we can embed new empowerment skills in all we do, making the behaviors aligned to psychological safety a habit, not just something we learn and then ignore.

We have differing levels of control across each of these approaches. We have a high level of control over the effort we exert to learn a new skill. We can influence, but not control how our team operates. And our ability to change our company culture is more likely to be out of our control or influence, but we can still support change over time. I will share tools during each stage of our journey together. You can then select from the tools available to you to create psychological safety over time for yourself, your team, and organization.

Psychological safety is difficult to visualize, since it exists in our heads and differs for each of us. So, I will use a visual from mountaineering to indicate a psychological safety tool you can consider using, and as a prompt for us to pause and reflect.

For those of you not familiar with mountain climbing, a carabiner is one of the more common pieces of safety equipment. It is small but mighty, commonly a 4-inch d-shaped piece of metal able to hold around 4,500 pounds when locked. While I heavily discourage trying it, a climbing carabiner could (in theory) hold some models of a Ford F-150 truck[13]. So, it is very well equipped to hold a 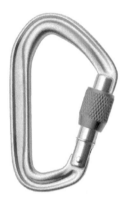 human's body weight. This is helpful when a climber is ascending a rock face and slips. The rope attached to the carabiner can save her life.

Carabiners are versatile.

A climber can use her carabiner to hold additional gear, often attached to her belt or harness. She can also attach a belay device to her carabiner, allowing her to repel down the mountain. She must trust her gear as she plants her feet firmly on the rock edge and leans backward over the cliff until the rope pulls tight to support her weight. If she has any fear of heights, a rush of adrenaline will flow through her as she commits to the descent, trusting her gear to stop her from plummeting to her death. But she will build confidence as she guides climbing rope through the carabiner and belay device, allowing her to safely descend to the bottom. When we first start to pursue psychological safety at work, we might feel a similar fear as the climber who first leans over the cliff and must trust her gear. As we continue to practice, we will also begin to trust the tools available to us and our fear will subside. Fear is normal and something we can work through.

When climbing with others, that same carabiner and belay device can be used to stop a friend from falling. A belayer is the person on the bottom of a rock-climbing wall who holds the rope as another person climbs. They can stop the climber from falling very far if she slips off the rock. Not surprisingly, this requires a lot of trust from the climber whose life is literally in the hands of the belayer. This is similar to how we might feel when we pursue psychological safety with our team. We need to trust each other if we hope to be vulnerable and share our ideas to achieve a common goal.

Carabiners can also enable new climbing routes up the rock face, particularly for something called traditional climbing. This is when a climber ascends a route that does not have any safety equipment attached to it. She must carry her own gear and attach safety equipment along the route, including a carabiner through which she can guide the rope as she climbs. She is not able to change the formation of the rock, but she can find new creative ways to ascend the face. This is how we might consider making changes across our company. We might not be able to shift how the company works in the short term, but we can begin to introduce new paths for achieving success.

How often do you speak up at work?

How do you think your coworkers would respond if you introduced a conversation about psychological safety?

CHAPTER 1:
HUMANS WANT TO FEEL SAFE

Meet Neo, an early Homo Sapiens from 100,000 years ago. Standing upright at five-and-a-half feet tall, his skull is a similar size and shape as current humans. Neo is fairly soft compared to other predators, which have a larger stature and integrated weapons, like large teeth and claws. Luckily Neo is smart and knows how to construct tools to make up for his natural deficiencies. He can shape rocks into sharp points and attach them to handles to create a spear[14.]

Also meet Kittie, the affectionately named leopard that lives in the same neighborhood as Neo. Kittie is no house cat. Instead of curling up on your lap, she prefers to eat you. Kittie loves eating humans[15.]

Although Kittie and Neo are comparable weights, she would outclass him in any wrestling match. Kittie prefers a close-up fight, stalking her prey until she can pounce and suffocate it by biting the neck. She then likes to enjoy her meal atop her favorite tree branches. Neo would be an easy target, if it wasn't for his pesky intelligence and tool-making ability.

Neo prefers to keep the fight at a distance. With the right planning and some luck, he can throw his spear into Kittie from afar, wait for her to die, and then eat her. No need for close-up combat.

For my meals, I prefer grocery shopping.

Until approximately 12,000 years ago, humans survived by hunting and gathering food. Like today, the human species could only continue if each individual safely secured enough food to sustain herself and enable the creation of more humans. Unlike today, they were at risk of dying when they captured their food. A leopard could lurk behind the next rock, ready to attack and kill the hunter. Over time, natural selection favored those who were able to avoid death by leopard and other threats. A key contributor to this survival was the ability to quickly identify and respond to a situation that requires fight-or-flight.

Fortunately, most of us do not still face this same life-threatening risk in the aisles of the grocery store. There are no leopards ready to pounce from behind the cereal boxes, but modern humans have retained the survival mechanism of our ancestors, ready to involuntarily and almost instantaneously activate our fight-or-flight feelings.

We are ready to avoid the leopard, although the leopard does not actually exist.

Our brain focuses on the immediate threat, driven by a desire for self-preservation and survival, and pushes other thoughts aside. All of this happens even when there is no physical threat, and often when we only feel a threat is possible, when it is just psychological.

Today, public speaking might cause the same fear as the leopard of the past.

The fear of public speaking is a non-generalized social anxiety disorder associated with performance situations that involve perceived scrutiny by others. It's the most common lifetime social fear, with more than one in five of us experiencing it. The fear of public speaking can be so intense that it causes psychological and physical symptoms, including shaking and panic attacks[16].

When we stand in front of the room, our survival response kicks in and our amygdala is hijacked. The amygdala is an almond-shaped structure in our brain. When it's activated, our heart rate rapidly increases, palms begin to sweat, and we're unable to think clearly. The amygdala overrides our cerebral cortex, the part of the brain that controls our logical reasoning, causing us to struggle to remember the speech we planned to deliver. The fear inhibits our ability to process complex thoughts, and instead defaults to our fight-or-flight instincts.

This might have served us well in the field with the leopard, as we were required to make quick decisions to ensure our survival, but this response is often unwelcome in our modern-day work and lives. We instead need to retain our ability to think clearly in complex situations.

Once we understand this connection between human history and brain functioning, it's easier for us to relate to the idea of psychological safety. Many of our brains respond similarly to a surprise leopard attack and standing in front of a large audience to deliver a speech. Phrased differently, our human desire for emotional or psychological safety is highly analogous to our desire for physical safety. This causes us to take actions, often unknowingly, to preserve our psychological safety. Just as we might flee a leopard, we might feel the desire to flee a stage, if our amygdala is triggered.

These psychological and physical response similarities extend beyond the amygdala hijack. Social psychologist Naomi Eisenberger found a correlation between brain responses to physical and emotional pain[17], hinting that our brains respond similarly to each type of pain. This calls into question the adage that "sticks and stones might break my bones, but words will never hurt me." While harmful words might not cause an observable wound on the outside of our bodies, the pain we experience is analogous to if someone threw a rock at us.

Just as we wouldn't tolerate physical violence at work, we'd be well served to create similar emotional safety in our workforce. Psychological safety allows each of us to speak up at any time, in the space that works best for us, with no feelings of risk or judgment. This isn't simply some fluffy stuff to make everyone feel good.

Psychological safety drives business performance across industries and was identified as the most important attribute for effective teams at Google.

In 2012, Google completed a study that spanned 180 global teams with thousands of surveys and hundreds of double-blind interviews, resulting in a summary analysis using 35 different statistical models across hundreds of variables[18]. The goal was to identify what makes an effective team. Google defined team effectiveness based on evaluations from executives, managers, and team members, in addition to sales performance against a quarterly quota. Surprising to many, the colocation of teams, team member extroversion, individual team member performance, workload size, seniority, team size, and tenure were not significantly connected to team effectiveness.

A single variable outweighed all others for driving effective teams—psychological safety.

For this analysis, Google defined psychological safety as "... a belief that a team is safe for risk taking in the face of being seen as ignorant, incompetent, negative, or disruptive. In a team with high psychological safety, teammates feel safe taking risks around their team members." The fear of the leopard attack is absent on these high performing teams, and we have more than twenty years of data to reinforce this finding.

Harvard's Amy Edmondson is a leader in this space, first publishing an academic paper about psychological safety in late 1999 and continuing to research it across global organizations. Spurred by her research in the medical profession, where she found better teams made more mistakes than their underperforming counterparts, Dr. Edmondson uncovered a surprising phenomenon.

High performing teams and companies are more likely to speak openly about failures, errors, and concerns without risk of repercussions[19.] This safety empowers individuals, teams, and organizations to proactively and openly identify potential challenges and work toward ongoing improvements. These feelings of psychological safety are likely to differ across teams within an organization, influenced significantly by the environment created by leadership.

 What do you consider to be the largest driver of team success at work? What role does psychological safety play?

The benefits of psychological safety, and the risks associated with failing to establish psychological safety, are consistent and repeatable. This doesn't only apply to massive tech companies like Google, but across industries. The public failures of Volkswagen, Wells Fargo, and Nokia provide a few of many cautionary examples of failures which could likely have been avoided by a culture filled with psychological safety.[20] In its absence, results can be disastrous.

In 2015, car manufacturer Volkswagen was caught manipulating the data outputs from their diesel engines, so their diesel engines could bypass emissions regulations and sell more cars. The discovery of this emissions cheating device, which made the engines falsely look as if they were achieving high fuel efficiency with low emissions of diesel pollutants, led to the recall of 8.5 million cars[21] and nearly $35 billion in fines and settlements[22].

The Wells Fargo banking scandal started when leadership set and aggressively pushed for unattainable sales targets, resulting in millions of fake accounts being built for unknowing customers. Wells Fargo had to pay $3 billion in penalties[23] and work diligently to regain customer trust.

Nokia is a slightly different story, with no scandals to cause their downfall, but a resistance to change that resulted in significant market losses. Once the market leader for handheld devices, Nokia failed to effectively adjust their strategy to account for Android and iOS competitors. This failure to adjust to the market forces was driven by leadership bureaucracy that inhibited sharing and implementation of new ideas across the organization[24].

Each of these companies shared a common flaw at the time of their downfall: a lack of psychological safety.

Engineers at Volkswagen unsuccessfully tried to share with leadership their concerns that it wouldn't be possible to create a diesel engine with low gas mileage that would pass emissions inspections. Branch managers at Wells Fargo failed in their attempts to express serious concern about the ability to cross-sell more products to customers. And Nokia maintained a culture of fear, where middle managers felt unable to share the impending negative news that they were unable to compete effectively with Apple and Google. While no single shift in company culture can fix everything, psychological safety would have helped to support better outcomes.

In a psychologically safe environment, leadership could have met with Volkswagen engineers, proactively asked about their concerns, challenged them to achieve greatness with the diesel engines, but then adjusted their expectations after multiple attempts indicated the timing and expectations were unachievable.

At Wells Fargo, an anonymous survey to branch employees could have easily uncovered what was happening, allowing leadership to openly discuss current targets and align on more reasonable growth expectations to match the company's goals with customers' needs.

Instead of remaining silent, Nokia employees could have proactively identified the challenges of their operating system versus the competitor's. They could have collaborated with leadership to try to establish a roadmap to success.

Psychological safety alone can't account for all of these potential positive outcomes, but it is easy to imagine how results would have changed in a psychologically safe environment. Leadership could have listened to the feedback from those around them and adjusted their strategy appropriately. Instead, employees were either ignored or silenced, resulting in potentially avoidable company failures.

The opposite consistently holds true; high psychological safety correlates with business success.

We also have several examples of success aligned with high psychological safety. High psychological safety increases collaboration and productivity, with a more engaged workforce that reports higher life satisfaction, lower stress, and accelerated skill development[25].

Pixar is exemplar in its invitation for a creative process full of candor[26,27]. With several box office hits like *Toy Story*, *The Incredibles*, and *Finding Nemo*, Pixar has grossed nearly $15 billion since 1995. Bob Iger is the CEO of Disney at the time of writing, previously acting as CEO from 2005 through 2020. He oversaw the acquisition of Pixar and describes it as his "proudest decision" as CEO, with Pixar leading the revitalization of Disney animation[28].

Pixar's creative development helped to drive this blockbuster success with a replicable approach to making movies we love. They institutionalized a way to create excellence through candid conversations, called the Braintrust. These meetings are intentionally designed to remove fear and create space for open discussions for improvement.

Pixar removed the fear of providing feedback by focusing the discussion on the movie's success, not the individual, or hidden personal agendas.

The Braintrust is a space that encourages attendees to let go of their fear of speaking up. It also creates a space that allows criticism to be received without a feeling of being attacked. Everyone in the Braintrust shares a goal of creating the best possible movie, and they know all movies are not good in the beginning. The journey to achieve movie greatness requires repeated iterations and feedback, even when that feedback might feel challenging.

The Braintrust acknowledges the best leaders and visionaries will also become lost sometimes. Even the movie's director collects feedback in the Braintrust. She reviews the feedback and then makes the final decision. So, there is also clear decision-making, aligned to a welcoming feedback process. Everyone is there to help make a great movie, presumably with no personal agendas.

The Braintrust models psychological safety. It creates the space for open dialogue and feedback, has a singular goal to make a great movie, and it has clear decision-making principles to allow everyone to move forward collectively.

Just as Pixar created the Braintrust to support the creation of blockbuster movies, Starbucks opened the 20,000 square-foot Tryer

Center to quickly test and iterate new drinks and operational improvements.

Since opening in November 2018, Starbucks' goal is to go from an idea to implementation in less than 100 days[29]. Starbucks was originally positioned as the "third place" for people to go between home and work. It was intended to be a place for people to enjoy their coffee in an uplifting environment that created a sense of community and gathering. But the company had to adjust this approach to align to customer needs.

In 2019, 80 percent of Starbucks orders were to-go[30]. Customers for only 20 percent of orders were embracing the "third place" and gathering in the store. In addition, cold beverages were outselling hot beverages, and these cold beverages were more time-intensive to make.

Starbucks' leadership recognized this shift and created a process to support improvement. While the process differs from Pixar's Braintrust, the Tryer Center invites a similar dialogue. Starbucks employees are invited to identify problems and opportunities, and to proactively find solutions. This requires the psychological safety to assert the existing process and Starbuck's menu can be better. It also requires Starbucks' leadership to recognize they don't have all the answers. They must invite ideas from the Starbucks partners, the name for Starbucks employees, to be the best company they can be.

In the first 18 months of opening the Tryer Center, Starbucks pursued 130 projects. This included new drinks, operational improvements, and ideas to support partners in their work. They've also tried to improve global partner inclusion for idea acquisition with Springboard, an internal company website that allows partners to share ideas and vote on projects.

Starbucks' $116-billion market cap[31] is eight times larger than competitor Peet's Coffee[32], nine times larger than the last known valuation of Dunkin' and Baskin-Robbins[33] combined, and 22 times larger than drive-through coffee chain Dutch Bros Coffee[34]. The company has also sustained year-over-year annual revenue growth from 2010 through 2022, except for the COVID-19 pandemic impact in 2020[35]. Starbucks' has achieved this financial success through a combination of its delicious products, fun seasonal offerings, great in-person experience, easy to use app, and commitment to stellar customer service. But the company continues to differentiate and grow, at least in part, because leadership realizes it does not have all the answers. They have created the systems to improve their products and customer experience, and they embrace feedback for ongoing improvement.

This idea of open dialogue based on psychological safety might feel foreign to many successful organizations, where a clear hierarchy with top-down decision-making is more of the norm. Even those environments can benefit from psychological safety. Considered one of the most hierarchical organizations, with life and death decisions made regularly in and during preparation for battle, the US Army would never care about psychological safety. Right? You might be surprised!

Major Kimberly Brutsche and Captain Tiarra McDaniel of the US Army also recognize the importance of psychological safety[36], recommending leaders create a culture of trust where individuals can speak up or take action without fear. To achieve this, they encourage soldiers to identify and address psychological dangers which often arise from an individual's fear of repercussions or losing acceptance within their group. They recognize psychological safety starts at the individual, with a focus on self-awareness and vulnerability. The leaders must provide support to individuals and teams, and the organization is responsible for creating the culture that embraces these discussions.

While shifting a culture to support psychological safety might be challenging, the underlying principles are surprisingly simple. We can achieve this with an invitation from leadership to share ideas, followed by a genuine and open dialogue with active listening on both sides. We must start with a foundation of trust.

 What is the first step you can take to create an environment that invites ideas from team members, without fear?

Start with Trust

In biology, there is a phrase called *mutualistic relationships*. In these relationships, the organisms work together to achieve benefits for both individuals. One of the more interesting mutualistic relationships occurs between moray eels and cleaner shrimp. Moray eels can be large, often around five feet long when fully grown[37]. They use their large teeth to tear flesh and grasp slippery prey, eating mostly small fish, crabs, and octopuses.

The moray eel could easily eat a two-inch-long cleaner shrimp, but instead, he lets the shrimp swim freely through his mouth and take nutrients from his razor-sharp teeth.

Pacific cleaner shrimp are brightly colored, with a band of red and white across their backs. They play a key role in coral reef ecosystems, with much of their diet coming from dead tissue and parasites they find on other fish. Often found in pairs, they set up cleaning stations within the corral and then perform a side-to-side rocking motion to indicate they are available to clean other fish[38]. Imagine a car wash with someone dancing out front to invite the cars in.

The difference is the cleaner shrimp often enters a predator's mouth to complete the cleaning! They risk their lives to collect food from the teeth of moray eels.

In this process, the cleaner shrimp gains nutrients from the body and teeth of the eel, removing and eating dead skin and parasites. The eel gains the benefit of a cleaner body and teeth, enhancing his ability to heal and reducing the risk of parasitic infection[39].

While it could be a stretch to apply the human construct of trust to animals beyond humans, this relationship between shrimp and eel models what we would describe as trust. The shrimp demonstrates vulnerability and enters a predator's mouth with the expectation they will not be eaten. The eel expects that the shrimp will eat the parasites that would otherwise do him harm. Both receive a benefit from a relationship that depends on the other following through on their expected behavior, consistent with what they demonstrated in prior interactions.

Trust is the base of our high functioning relationships[40]. We can build trust when we show up as capable and competent, follow through on what we say, and demonstrate empathy. We can also quickly reduce trust when we regularly focus on our personal gain, without considering the impact on others[41].

There are many ways to identify and define trust, but in this case, we will accept the definition that incorporates vulnerability and positive expectations. Like the cleaner shrimp and moray eel, trust within our working teams develops when we are genuinely vulnerable, working in support of others while achieving our personal goals. As humans, we can begin to demonstrate this vulnerability through self-disclosure. When done correctly and modeled by others, each team member will begin to recognize it is acceptable for them to also share ideas, which helps to reinforce the team trust[42]. We believe the statements and behaviors shared by others, with positive expectations of others' actions. Through this trust, each team member embraces failure as temporary and an option to learn and applauds successes for themselves and others.

When you have trust, the team is more likely to be conscientious and courteous, with improved job satisfaction, commitment to the organization and to leadership decisions, while reducing interest in pursuing other jobs[43]. These teams are better equipped to engage in productive conflict, commit to their work, and be accountable for the outcomes as they pursue their goals. Similar to psychological safety, employees in high-trust companies report lower stress, higher energy, and increased productivity[44]. When teams trust their leaders, everyone feels more confident and comfortable discussing all aspects of work, even the problems that arise. They know their manager and teammates will operate with the best intentions.

Psychological safety relies heavily on trust, since our comfort speaking up in difficult situations relies on our belief that others won't judge us. As a result, it is easy to feel we can refer to trust and psychological safety as the same thing. But they are different concepts. We experience psychological safety in a moment when we assess our comfort speaking up or try something new. Trust is more aligned to future expectations, with previous experiences helping us predict how others will interact with us.

Trust is the basis from which psychological safety can thrive. We need to keep trust top of mind, as we consider how we can best build psychological safety within our teams and organizations.

In what relationships do you feel the most trust?

How can you replicate that feeling of trust with your team at work?

Avoid Pampering and Aggression

Psychological safety is not constant positivity, nor is it an invitation to berate others with uncaring criticism. When we have psychological safety we are more apt to share compliments when justified. We also more easily acknowledge and discuss personal feelings. We collaborate to achieve our common and individual goals. We provide feedback and criticism with a desire to help others improve over time, anchoring in genuine care. This balance might feel challenging as we try to provide positive feedback without pampering and provide criticism without acting with aggression.

Figure 1: Psychological safety requires a balance of positive feedback and criticism.

Our brains are a lot like our bodies.

If we were pampered with massages, relaxation on the couch, naps anytime we want, all our favorite foods and no exercise, we might feel great for a couple days. But if we continued this relaxation for a few weeks, our muscles would start to atrophy. Over time, they would begin to break down and lose strength, increasing the likelihood of heart failure and diabetes[45].

Our ability to deal with emotional and psychological stressors–our emotional strength–also atrophies if we are only pampered and never challenged. This is part of why cognitive behavioral therapy (CBT) encourages people to face their fears and practice responding to them, not avoid them[46]. CBT is a well-researched approach to support improvement for many psychological challenges. Avoiding emotional challenges is like physical pampering. Both lead to weakness and reduced ability to respond to stimulus effectively.

The opposite is also true. Our bodies struggle to adapt to aggressive exercise that regularly exceeds our current ability. When we work out too much, we are more likely to experience ongoing muscle or joint pain, an increased heart rate, an inability to relax, difficulty sleeping, and more frequent illness. Our bodies have limits and these symptoms are our bodies' way of telling us to take a break.

Similarly, we emotionally break down when exposed to a psychologically aggressive workplace. When we experience aggression at work, we are more likely to perform worse on our job-related tasks and to contribute less to the overall organization[47]. Psychological aggression causes us to perform worse.

As we pursue psychological safety for ourselves, our teams, and organizations, we might sometimes accidentally dedicate too much effort toward positive reinforcement. At other times, we might accidentally act in a way that others perceive as aggressive. Each of us will make mistakes or misread situations, and we can then learn and improve over time. As we work through this journey, watch for the moments where you are pampering someone with praise, and consider how you could better support them with a more critical assessment to help them improve. And watch for the moments where your focus on problems has made it difficult for the team to find the bright spots. If you catch yourself in these moments, you can then begin to adjust toward a more balanced approach of praise and supportive criticism.

In the last week, how many compliments did you provide to members of your team? How many critiques?

Consider asking the people with whom you work most closely: How is my balance of compliments versus sharing ideas to improve? How can I show up better?

CHAPTER 2:
YOU MATTER

Our individual experiences and identity are key components of psychological safety, directly influencing our comfort levels for sharing ideas with others. Women, particularly those who identify as LGBTQ+, Black, or disabled are more likely than their peers to experience subtle or unintentional discrimination. This is often referred to as microaggression. Compared to their male peers, they are more likely to be interrupted and have their judgment questioned[48]. This is all despite repeated global findings across 1,000 large companies that show increased gender and ethnic diversity in the employee pool correlates with a higher likelihood of financial performance exceeding that of peer companies[49].

Each of us experiences the world differently based on our prior experiences and worldview. For example, an upper-middle class, cisgender, politically conservative, White male with a master's degree in Computer Science likely has a different experience with the world than a trans-gender, politically liberal, Black woman from a low socio-economic status and a Master of Sociology. Both can be well intentioned and very strong at their jobs but the data show that the White male is less likely to experience microaggression or have his ideas questioned. Due to systemic and repeated bias, often unconscious, the White male is more likely to have had positive work experiences that allow him to feel more comfortable speaking up. He's more likely to feel psychologically safe than the Black woman, even in the same meeting and work environment.

Acknowledging these differences creates the opportunity for us to discuss them openly, which helps establish an environment of psychological safety. In 2015, I founded and co-led an initiative at Google called Relate, alongside other managers in my working group. Our goal was to understand the disparate experiences of the individuals on our teams so we could better support them. We hoped to establish a level of understanding and comfort that would allow everyone to speak openly about our challenges, limitations, and opportunities for growth, in support of our personal and team success. While many organizations have already conducted and shared research about underrepresented individuals in the workforce, we wanted to build on that knowledge with conversations that allowed us to create better connections with those around us.

My working group aligned on four topics to discuss, including: those from families with income that did not meet their needs, non-US cultures, underrepresented ethnicities, and female identity. The topics we selected often had a significant influence on each impacted individual, but they were not intended to define or stereotype anyone. We followed a five-step process for each topic.

1.   *Acknowledge.* Each of us has a combination of experiences and influences in our lives, and it is rare for any single attribute to

define who we are or to be universal in its influence. For example, we didn't assume that everyone who came from a non-US culture experienced their move to the United States in the same way. We were always careful to not stereotype or assume anything about an individual. We also proactively acknowledged these conversations might feel challenging. We didn't want any individuals to feel a burden to represent a group with which they identified, and we attempted to openly communicate and address these feelings.

2. *Understand.* We conducted one-to-one interviews with individuals on the team who identified with the selected topics to learn their perspective and how it influenced their work. We approached the interviews with high sensitivity, not presuming anyone identified with the topics we identified. We invited everyone on the team to participate, and then conducted the discussions with team members who showed high interest. We anonymously documented the discussions and identified consistent themes.

3. *Create.* We then created a brief presentation with common takeaways from these discussions, all with permission from those who shared their perspective. These presentations were used as discussion guides with the leadership team.

4. *Discuss.* The leadership team then dedicated 60 minutes per topic to review the common takeaways, share our personal experiences, and begin to consider steps we can take to create a more inclusive and successful environment for everyone on our teams. These discussions were so heartfelt that leaders were sometimes brought to tears as they considered the challenges experienced by those around us.

5. *Share.* This final stage is crucial. At this point, we had openly discussed personal experiences with team members, aggregated their feedback, and started to discuss ideas to improve as a leadership team. The next step was to enact change in support of our teams and leadership and this entailed three actions. Each manager led sessions with their teams to share the process we followed. We shared some of the anonymous findings and our ideas to improve and invited an ongoing open dialogue with feedback. Wherever we identified a need for systemic improvements, we shared our findings and recommendations with senior leadership and human resources. I then shared our approach with other managers so they could replicate it with their teams, but with topics they selected that would be most relevant to their needs.

Our leadership group learned of several powerful individual perceptions within our teams that were aligned to their experiences and backgrounds with the four topics we had discussed.

Low Income

Those who identified as coming from families with income that did not meet their needs shared similar stories about having to send money to family members, with some of their parents expecting the new-college graduate Googler to pay many of the parents' expenses. In these situations, where the Googler might be the only person in the family with a college degree and high paying job, the pressure and expectation to support the family can be overwhelming. In some cases, the Googler struggled to pay their own bills, take vacations, or save for retirement because they gave much of their money to family. As a result of this burden and expectation to support others, there was a consistent feeling among this group that they should not take risks at work or speak up too much. Instead, they should remain quiet and follow the rules. Their priority was to do their best at their core role.

Underrepresented Ethnicities

We learned of a similar risk aversion when we spoke to those who identified with underrepresented ethnicities, predominately Black and Indian. In my discussions with Black team members and leadership, I heard stories of parents teaching their children from a young age to not challenge authority, to be compliant and complete their work without complaint. This sadly arises largely from historical and current context and racially motivated discrimination and abuse within the United States. The impact at work is similar to those who grew up in a lower socioeconomic status, with the Black team members less likely to speak up or challenge leadership.

Non-US Cultures

Our team members from non-US cultures shared a different reason for not speaking up. They often did not understand the context or references within our training, business, or happy hour discussions. This particularly impacted our team members who moved to the United States from India, but also those who moved from Europe and elsewhere. For example, American football and baseball references used to be common in sales training. Our Indian teammates would sometimes struggle to immediately understand what we meant by "quarterbacking a meeting" or that a "sales pitch was a home run." These are things they can pick up over time and develop comfort discussing, but in the first months after a move to a new location, US-based references like those can be enough to cause a pause in a discussion, not allowing the voice of the non-US culture to be heard.

Female Identity

Female identity was the final group we met with, including those who were born female and anyone who identified as female. In these discussions, we heard concern that nearly all senior leadership was male and mostly White. It was difficult for the women on our teams to imagine rising to a senior leadership position when they didn't see role models that looked like them. This felt discouraging, and at times would cause them to feel less motivated and less likely to speak up.

All of these discussions shared a common result. Team members who came from families with income that didn't meet their needs, were members of an underrepresented ethnicity, weren't born in the United States, or identified as female were more reluctant to share their ideas. They were also less likely to challenge authority. These feelings weren't universal, but they were repeated and consistent. The *Relate* initiative opened the discussion and created the context for our leadership team to explore ways to improve the experience for these team members. All of this occurred without fear of humiliation or repercussions, but simply with a genuine desire to support those around us.

Relate reinforced the third-party research, helping our leadership team recognize how each of us experiences psychological safety differently, with those in underrepresented groups likely to feel less safe than those in the majority. *Relate* also caused me and others to further reflect about our relationship with psychological safety—how we create it for others and ourselves.

After piloting *Relate* within our team of approximately 150, I then supported the expansion across multiple other sales teams within the United States, Canada, and South America. Each team slightly customized the approach to support their regional and cultural needs. As with many of these types of projects, we made a brief positive impact on our teams and others, but this kind of work needs to be recurring and across a company to maintain impact.

How can you start a conversation with your team to better understand each individual's experiences and how those experiences impact their contributions to work?

What topics could you consider discussing with your team to support psychological safety for everyone, not just the dominant culture?

CHAPTER 3:
INVITE, SHARE, AND LISTEN

March 27, 1977, was the date of the deadliest plane crash in aviation history.

On that foggy morning, two planes intended to take off from a Las Palmas airport runway on the Spanish island of Tenerife. Tenerife is the largest of the Canary Islands, a grouping of seven main and several smaller islands. The 644 passengers on KLM Flight 4805 and Pan Am Flight 1736 never intended to visit Tenerife. But they were diverted after a separatist political group detonated a bomb at their original destination on the Canary Island of Gran Canaria.

These flights and others were diverted to Las Palmas to ensure passenger safety.

Las Palmas was a small airport though, with only one runway, one main taxiway, and four smaller taxiways to connect the others. So, the diverted planes filled the taxiways, forcing pilots to taxi planes within the runway. This congestion led to riskier takeoffs and landings, as pilots tried to avoid other planes in the vicinity.

The KLM cockpit crew consisted of Captain Veldhuyzen van

Zanten, First Officer Klaas Meurs, and Flight Engineer Willem Schreuder. The captain had three times more experience with the 747 they were flying, compared to the first officer and flight engineer. The tower instructed the KLM flight crew to taxi to takeoff position. The crew performed their checklist and intended to announce their readiness before they departed.

The tower then asked the Pan Am flight crew to enter the third taxiway. The crew saw the first two taxiways, but they struggled to identify the third due to heavy fog. By the time the Pan Am flight reached the runway, they had reported visibility of 100 meters, only 20 percent of when they started the takeoff process. These poor conditions caused them to turn onto the wrong taxiway, placing them in the center of the runway ahead of the KLM flight.

A variety of communication challenges followed, all recorded before the accident. Perhaps most importantly, Captain van Zanten ignored his first officer's and engineer's cautions against beginning the taking off process. First Officer Meurs told Captain van Zanten they did not have clearance from the tower for takeoff, but van Zanten continued to advance the throttles. Instead of waiting for approvals, the captain ignored the less experienced first officer and attempted to gain clearance as the plane moved down the runway.

As they gained speed, Flight Engineer Schreuder asked the cockpit to confirm the Pan Am flight was clear of the runway. Captain van Zanten replied with his last words, "Oh, yes" and attempted to continue takeoff[50]. The KLM plane drove directly into the Pan Am plane, which sat amidst the fog on the same runway.

583 people died.

Many factors led to this tragic event. A regional airport was overwhelmed by more planes than normal, filling the taxiways and runway. The fog made it impossible to see the full runway. Some of the communication between the tower and flight crews appears to have been misunderstood. The Pan Am flight took the wrong taxiway. But the primary factor was the KLM captain continuing to accelerate down a runway, despite not gaining clearance from the tower. If he had not pushed the throttle, the lives would not have been lost.

Despite the first officer and flight engineer warning against takeoff, the captain still moved forward.

Like 19 of 20 airline accidents, the Tenerife tragedy was caused by human error. A follow up study found three major contributors to the accident: stress, small group communication, and small group dynamics[51]. The high-risk situation of taking off from a foggy and busy runway increased stress, impairing their ability to consider alternative approaches.

The cockpit crew behavior also aligns well with a discussion about psychological safety. While there is no way to know the mindset of the captain, first officer, or engineer in the moments before takeoff, the call logs indicate low psychological safety. Nearly half of the major air transport disasters between 1978 and 1990 were a result of first officers not speaking up to captains. Captain van Zanten exhibited what could have been expected from the airline's hierarchical structure. He ignored or rejected the warnings he heard, as he took on centralized decision-making and shut out the less experienced co-workers.

If the flight crew had high psychological safety, perhaps the accident could have been avoided. Imagine if First Officer Meurs and Flight Engineer Schreuder were able to be more assertive in their statements. Instead of Schreuder asking a question, he could have made a direct statement to stop the takeoff. And Captain van Zanten could have listened, adjusted his approach and saved nearly 600 lives.

The principles of psychological safety would undoubtedly have helped here[52]. This could have included an invitation from the captain to discuss the takeoff, sharing of concerns by the cockpit crew, and delaying the takeoff until the concerns were addressed.

It is easy to review history and write a better outcome, and I do not intend to disparage anyone in the KLM or Pan Am crews, nor the Tenerife airport. I can only loosely imagine the stress they experienced in those final moments, along with the fatigue they must have felt after being diverted from their original destination due to a bombing, and the subsequent poor conditions at an overwhelmed small airport. Any of us could have made similar mistakes. This tragedy can help us reflect and learn though, to hopefully support others from avoiding similar mistakes.

The creation of psychological safety is not an exact science, but there are typically three essential components to its activation. We can invite a conversation, allow for open sharing, and actively listen (Figure 2). Through this exchange, we can then make more informed and better decisions.

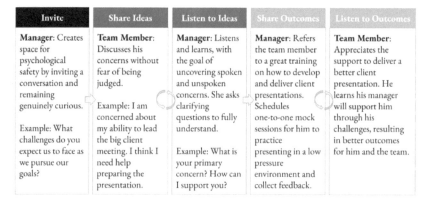

Invite	Share Ideas	Listen to Ideas	Share Outcomes	Listen to Outcomes
Manager: Creates space for psychological safety by inviting a conversation and remaining genuinely curious. Example: What challenges do you expect us to face as we pursue our goals?	**Team Member:** Discusses his concerns without fear of being judged. Example: I am concerned about my ability to lead the big client meeting. I think I need help preparing the presentation.	**Manager:** Listens and learns, with the goal of uncovering spoken and unspoken concerns. She asks clarifying questions to fully understand. Example: What is your primary concern? How can I support you?	**Manager:** Refers the team member to a great training on how to develop and deliver client presentations. Schedules one-to-one mock sessions for him to practice presenting in a low pressure environment and collect feedback.	**Team Member:** Appreciates the support to deliver a better client presentation. He learns his manager will support him through his challenges, resulting in better outcomes for him and the team.

Figure 2: The invitation to freely share ideas can occur during any meeting, allowing for a continuous cycle of sharing and listening to achieve the best outcome. This example includes a manager and team member, but anyone can begin the conversation.

1) Invite

The start of a conversation about how to improve a current approach or expand on previous success typically begins with an invitation. For some of us who are fortunate to already be in a highly trusting relationship with our manager and team, this invitation might have occurred nonverbally. We might have a shared understanding through the modeling of others that it is acceptable to speak up with our ideas. For the rest of us who are early in our journey toward psychological safety, where we do not yet feel comfortable sharing our ideas, we must verbalize this invitation.

The invitation can come from anyone on the team and has to be based on a genuine interest in learning.

At the start of each project and meeting, we can remind everyone involved that we want to hear their ideas for improvement, so we can fix avoidable problems as we work to achieve our goals. We also want to hear what is working well, so we can learn from others' success, helping us to reach and exceed our collective goals.

Invitation questions could look like these, but we should customize them to the context that fits our and our team's needs. What challenges do you expect us to face as we pursue our plan? How can we improve our approach? What is working well for us? How can others replicate this? Each of these questions provides the opportunity to consider alternatives. Even if everyone seems to be excited and aligned, we can prompt further reflection by asking: What potential problems might we face if we continue down this path?

Even when the invitation comes from a member of the team, leadership plays a crucial role. If leadership fails to allow the space to share and actively listen, the conversation will be stifled. If they support sharing and listen openly to consider alternative approaches, they will inspire future sharing and better outcomes.

2) Share Ideas + Listen

Sharing occurs in two phases. The first is the idea sharing in response to the invitation.

If a manager asks her team what challenges they expect to face as they pursue their goals, then the next step is for the team to share their ideas. They might share concerns they have with the strategy they are pursuing, their individual skill alignment to the team needs, the manager's communication style, a difficult customer relationship, or feelings related to the goal setting process from leadership. Since she has invited a discussion with thoughtful questions, she is likely to hear a variety of responses, some unexpected.

At this point in the process, the manager's role is simply to listen and learn. She is not ready to share her perspective or ideas until she collects the relevant feedback. She can instead try to ask thoughtful follow up questions to ensure she fully understands and monitor body language to try to assess if there is more to uncover than what the team members are saying. By fully engaging in listening, she is better equipped to form an informed opinion and response.

3) Share Outcomes + Listen

The next step is crucial. It is the moment when the manager, or whoever has received the idea, responds. Sometimes, it will make sense to change a strategy based on new information or feedback. Other times, we can be heard but the decision maker will determine it is still appropriate to continue down the original path. Both are reasonable responses.

This is also a moment of heightened sensitivity. As humans, we have evolved to care about interpersonal connections and often feel hurt, anxious, or embarrassed when we are personally rejected by others[53]. In my experience, we can also experience these feelings when our ideas are rejected. This is particularly true if we fail to understand how decisions are made or the context in which they are made. We will consider decision-making more in Part 3, but we will briefly review a reminder about perspective here.

Team members and managers often have different experiences and therefore arrive at different perspectives, even when looking at the same thing. The optical illusion of Old Woman Young Woman, first printed on a German postcard in 1888, is a great example of how we see

different things while viewing the same information. What do you see in the image at left?

Some will see a young woman with a petite nose glancing backward to the left. Others will see an elderly woman with a long chin looking forward, also to the left. Those who have seen this before might be able to transition between the images with some effort, seeing each at different times. Interestingly, if you are 30 years old or younger, you are more likely to see the young woman. If you are older than 30, you are more likely to see the older woman[54].

Our individual context and biases guide us toward different realities, and both can be correct. The same is true for decisions at work.

As the manager listens to the ideas from her team, her goal is to begin to see all perspectives, the young and elderly women in the same picture. She can acknowledge her biases toward her original perspective, consider others', and then share the path forward. At this point in the process, the manager will share the outcome of the discussion with her team and align toward next steps.

In a psychologically safe workplace, this process—invite, share, listen—repeats over time. Each conversation is an opportunity to invite larger conversations. This can happen in a weekly team or in one-to-one meetings, in new or in impromptu project planning sessions ... all or either, to ensure the team is following the best path forward. Each member of the team and the leadership must be committed to genuinely respond to the invitation, share ideas, and listen openly. They must be willing to adjust their personal perspective based on new information they learn.

Consider your current work goals, for yourself and your team.

Invite: What questions could you ask to collect honest feedback about how you can improve your current business operations?

Share: How can you create a safe space for yourself and others to share ideas?

Listen: What steps will you take to remain open to others' ideas?

PART TWO:

Personal Journey—

Establish the Basis for Psychological Safety

Nearly one-in-three of the 58 million Americans who exercise prefer walking over alternatives. They tend to walk alone, and they're more likely to go with family or friends when they decide to walk with others[55]. With each step, these walkers are losing weight, reducing their cravings for sweets, lowering their risk for cancer, easing pain, and boosting their immunity[56]. Not too shabby!

Now let's consider the logistics for an individual named Maria, who tries to walk daily. Maria has a full-time job and a family, so she has to get up at 5:30 in the morning to complete her walk, before the duties of the day interfere with her plans. She is healthy and capable of walking.

Most mornings, her alarm wakes her up from a sound sleep. She slowly wakes from her dream, rubs her eyes, takes a deep breath, and pauses to question the day's decision: To stay in bed under the covers and sleep another hour? Or to get out of bed and gain the benefit from the day's walk?

Only Maria determines what happens next. She decides if she will roll back onto her pillow for some extra sleep or lace up her shoes for the morning walk. She has full control over her actions.

Now let's mix it up. Maria's friend Paula has expressed interest in joining these morning walks. Paula knows she'll have to set an earlier alarm, but she promises to join the next time. Maria is excited to share the experience with Paula and she assumes they can hold each other accountable.

The next morning, Maria bounces out of bed with the expectation of walking with Paula. As Maria gets ready to step outside, Paula texts to say she's unsure if she can do it. She stayed up a little too late last night and hopes to get more sleep before a busy day at work.

At this moment, Maria can encourage Paula to join her, but she's not able to force her out of her house. She also doesn't have the full context for what Paula is experiencing or feeling. Maria wants to push Paula to join her so they can both gain the benefits from walking. But she also doesn't want to push Paula to do something she really doesn't want to do. The risks of forcing the issue could outweigh the benefits of having a partner for the walk. At this moment, Maria is dealing with her small team of two and determining the appropriate approach to influence Paula. She is no longer in full control of the situation.

Maria feels disappointed that Paula didn't join her, but she is not discouraged! Instead, she joins a local walking club with several hundred members, including a club leader who schedules all the outings. Maria knows she will lose much of the control she had when she walked alone, no longer able to make the decisions about when and where the group will walk. But she gains the camaraderie of the many like-minded walkers who live near her. They can teach her new walking routes, inform her about the best gear, and share fun adventure stories. She is willing to make the tradeoff of losing control in favor of building relationships and sharing her walks with others.

Maria's story serves as a model for how this book will flow. We will start with each of us as Individuals, where we have the most control, just as when Maria walked alone. We will then consider how we can expand our influence, with a focus on our working Team. This is like when Maria tried to walk with Paula. We will then consider our larger Organization, which most of us are unable to control or influence in the short term, just as Maria joined a walking group for which others made most decisions.

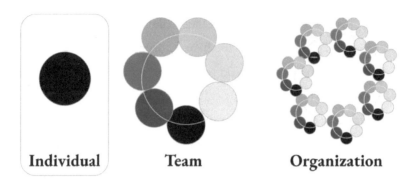

Individual   **Team**   **Organization**

Individual

The journey toward psychological safety starts within each of us.

Each of us is responsible for our actions and how we respond to situations. Assuming there are no legitimate external factors inhibiting us from acting, we are in control of what we do physically and how we respond emotionally. I can choose to sleep in or wake up early to start my work for the day. I can decide how I react to an email I perceive as aggressive. I can decide if I want to push my own agenda or give a voice to others.

This part of the book will focus on how we can begin our personal journey to embrace psychological safety. We will acknowledge that learning new skills can be challenging and will consider how our motivation, mentality, and environment can support our progress. We will consider the path many of us will follow along this journey and a framework for how we can become more comfortable sharing ideas at work.

Those of us who share our ideas and are heard are more likely to feel engaged at work and experience higher job satisfaction[57]. When everyone is included in these conversations, the team thrives.

Team

After we've started to build our personal approach to supporting psychological safety, we're then prepared to bring these conversations to our teams. We will spend the most time here.

The definition of a work team can sometimes be nebulous, since we often work closely with a few people but rely on many to achieve our goals. We'll consider a team to be a group of people who pursue interdependent tasks in support of achieving a common objective.

Since our team is the group of people with whom we have the most interactions, we can likely influence our team members, just as they influence us. When we can freely speak up and share ideas, we not only have an improved working experience, but also positively impact the team. We are able to provide ideas for improvement and share our successes so everyone in our working group can be lifted. Our positive feelings about our working environment also translate to others through better interpersonal connections and a concept called "emotional contagion." Emotional contagion describes when we mimic the feelings and actions of those around us, helping to make us feel good when our teammates feel good and vice-versa. We'll explore emotional contagion in a little more detail later.

Part 3 of this book will guide us through ways we can consider building psychological safety within our working teams, with ongoing open communication. We'll consider how we can create personal connections through stories, shared learning, and empathy-building. These connections can also help us succeed with our business goals, as we rally around a common purpose, align on decision-making, and clearly articulate next steps. We'll help to ensure ongoing commitment and improvement through coaching, feedback, and behavior modeling.

Organization

Unless we work for a small company or hold an executive role, most of us aren't in positions to control or influence our organizational culture in the short-term. But each of us can positively impact organizational culture over time. Part 4 of this book will consider ways we can expand our impact beyond ourselves and our working team through surveys, independent projects, and the open embrace of differences.

Our ability to control and influence often changes over time. These abilities can shift as we change roles, gain promotions, get a new manager, experience a company reorganization, or move to a new company.

We'll start by focusing on ourselves, since our effort and emotions are likely the only things within our work that we can fully and directly control. With the right mindset, patience to try and fail, and understanding of ourselves and some key concepts from psychology, we will set ourselves up to have the psychological safety we want at work. Through this focus on ourselves to start, we'll be better equipped to model positive and open communication and will gain the language to use in discussions with others. By building our confidence about the conversation, we're more likely to feel safe speaking up.

What holds you back from sharing ideas for improvement at work?

What steps can you take to feel more confident sharing your ideas?

CHAPTER 4:
BE PATIENT. GROWTH IS DIFFICULT.

Brushing your teeth is probably one of the most mindless parts of your day, but it wasn't always that way.

For the hundredth time, I pick up the toothbrush made for a mini-human, complete with cartoon characters and my two-year-old son's favorite colors. I dabble the slightest amount of fluoride toothpaste onto the bristles and take a deep breath to try to remain calm as I embark on one of the most challenging parts of my day. I somehow have to guide those sudsy bristles over my son's teeth, preferably without injury to him or me, and with the least running and screaming possible from either of us. All of this tends to happen during the morning hours, when time is scarce as we try to get out the door to required activities for the day, or when we're all exhausted at night.

The game is consistent with each brushing attempt. First, he must hold the toothbrush and try to clean his own teeth. This usually consists of him biting the brush, laughing and squirming from my arms to run laps around the second floor of our home. My desire to catch this rabid child is matched with a fear of him running directly into a wall or falling flat on his face and jamming the toothbrush into the back of his throat, requiring us to go to the Emergency Room. Thus far, we've avoided the toothbrush-induced ER.

When I finally catch him, I provide a courteous count to ten and ask him to pass the toothbrush to me. Ten ... 9 ... 8 ... 7 ... 6 ... 5 ... 4 ... 3 ... 2 ... CRASH! Like clockwork, he throws the toothbrush past my grasping hand into anything nearby. I now have to hold him in one hand as I slowly dip with a struggling groan to pick up the toothbrush with the other.

I wash the toothbrush in the sink and try again.

But he's too smart for me. He knows I can't put a toothbrush in his mouth if both his hands are in there. So, he shoves two hands as far into his mouth as possible and shakes his head to avoid the cleaning. He shrills happily through all of this, knowing I'll eventually break down too and start laughing at the insanity. It's much more fun to laugh than let the tears of frustration flow.

And we're just trying to do this simple routine of brushing teeth!

The thing is, this routine isn't simple for my 2-year-old son. It's a fun game with a colorful toy (the toothbrush), some fun flavors (the toothpaste), a ride of sorts (running around and me picking him up), and culminating with some laughter (I'm a sucker for cuteness). We eventually clean as many of those teeth as possible, but it's a journey to get there.

Like many habits we develop in life, brushing our teeth likely started as more of a challenge, requiring mental energy and effort to remember to merge the water, toothpaste, and toothbrush through our mouths to avoid cavities and improve our breath. But as adults, we think nothing of it. We can easily brush our teeth without thinking deeply about what we're doing. We can daydream about other activities or even try to multitask while brushing. The thing that was originally difficult has become embedded in our behavior, occurring without us thinking about it.

Developing a new skill is often challenging. Only after repeated practice over time, and with many failures along the way, can even the most seemingly simple tasks become habits. We will explore this habit development in Part 5 of this book, but we'll first focus on how we can approach the start of learning new things.

For most new behaviors we learn, we must first go through a period that might sometimes feel uncomfortable.

If learning to brush our teeth felt challenging, it's reasonable to assume improving our feelings of psychological safety will require significant effort. And just as learning the skill of teeth brushing reaped the rewards of a clean mouth, improved health and fresh breath, the skill of building psychological safety reaps many benefits. Individuals feel more empowered and happier. Teams become more effective. Companies are set up to thrive. The skill development might feel challenging, but each of us is capable!

The National Academies of Sciences, Engineering, and Medicine collaborated on a decades-long review of how humans learn, expanding on a similar effort from twenty years earlier. The cumulative knowledge spans four decades and encompasses findings from across three professional disciplines[58].

Learning is a complex process that is influenced by our culture, social interactions, cognitive development, and biology. As a result, each of us experiences learning in slightly different ways. But we also share some similarities.

Conscious learning requires sustained effort. To maintain our effort and adopt new behaviors, we must want to learn. We must be motivated to continue to try to improve and grow, even when it is difficult, or we won't gain conscious learning. When our motivation, mentality, and environment work together we are more likely to maintain our journey of ongoing improvement (Figure 3).

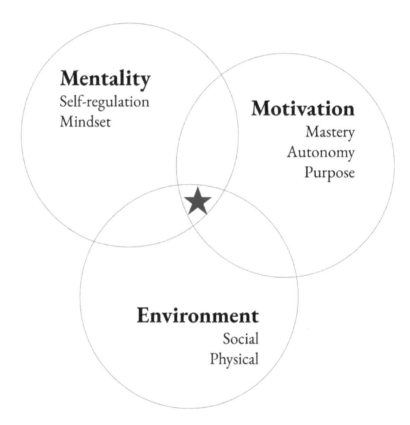

Figure 3: Our motivation, mentality, and environment contribute significantly to our ability to learn and adopt a new skill.

Motivation

Our motivation is impacted by many things like our upbringing, past experiences, cultural and societal norms, beliefs, and environment. Through these experiences we identify goals we want to achieve in our lives. Some motivators are external, imposed on us by an outside system like school, work, or society. Others are internal, created by us as a means to feel fulfilled with our life pursuits.

The most common motivation analogy is that of the carrot and stick. When your manager rewards you with a bonus for exceeding a sales goal, she's using the carrot. When she provides a disciplinary performance review for repeatedly missing your goals, she's using the stick. The carrot and stick can sometimes work well for short term goals, like the sales contest to reward a top performer. The extra bonus might inspire a short-term spurt of additional activity and effort, but these gains are often temporary. They focus on a single outcome that must be repeated and often expanded, if the manager hopes to gain the same positive response from her team. To gain the same positive outcome, the manager will likely need to increase the size of the reward in the future, if she intends to continue using the carrot for motivation.

This type of motivation is called extrinsic. As a manager or team member partnering with others, it's easy to default to extrinsic motivators because there is a clear definition of win versus loss, but this easier tactic isn't always best.

The National Academy of Sciences encourages educators to consider other approaches to maintain motivation. Motivation will be highest when learning is aligned to an experience the learner values, where they have control and autonomy, where they can recognize their progress, and where they feel well supported throughout the learning journey. In his best-selling book *Drive*, Dan Pink provides a similar argument to expand our thinking beyond the carrot and stick in favor of promoting mastery, autonomy, and purpose[59], which provide more sustained motivation and align us toward intrinsic motivators.

Intrinsic motivation is internal, based on self-fulfillment, personal satisfaction, and accomplishment. We're more likely to continue pursuing a challenging effort like building psychological safety if we're motivated intrinsically. We're more likely to be successful if we find an approach that allows us to continue to learn and feel a sense of personal contribution, and if we become aligned to a purpose we believe in. We tend to be intrinsically motivated by things we care most about and are more likely to continue to pursue them, even in the absence of external reinforcement.

This is not to say we need to focus only on intrinsic motivation, but to seriously consider the balance of how we motivate ourselves and others, likely with more of a focus on intrinsic. Most of us enjoy receiving praise for work well done or the occasional bonus for surpassing expectations. But if we rely too heavily on these rewards, we can lose track of the source of our original motivation. Too many monetary bonuses can actually harm our intrinsic motivation[60], especially when those bonuses are expected[61]. Instead of money, we can provide praise and positive social reinforcement to maintain commitment toward the goal.

As we pursue psychological safety for ourselves and others, we're more likely to remain committed if we understand our purpose, maintain some autonomy to pursue improvements, and can see ongoing improvement. For me, this purpose goes back to my goals since a young age. For as long as I can remember, I've wanted to do good for others while pursuing a successful career that would allow me to live comfortably. This aligns well with psychological safety since it builds on a base of helping others feel comfortable sharing their ideas. Those shared ideas support business success. This journey will never end for me, since I can always improve and suspect I will never achieve mastery of this topic.

Each reader will have to consider their purpose in this journey, how they will measure success, and what they aspire to achieve. We can think of the journey as being both in support of ourselves and those around us.

Things do not always go as planned, so even with the strongest motivation, each of us will need to be deliberate in our ongoing dedication to our purpose. Our mentality can help to keep us on track.

Mentality

Learning and building new habits is complex and we can easily be diverted from our goals, even when we have strong motivation. Consider December 31st, New Year's Eve, the time of the year when people in the United States are most likely to make a commitment to change. The transition to a new year is a great prompt to reflect on the previous year and consider ways to improve moving forward. Even with that strong desire to make a change or learn something new, nine of ten people fail to follow through[62]. Strava, a popular app for athletes to track their workouts around the world, analyzed millions of January activities and identified the day when people are likely to break their goal. So many people abandon their New Years resolutions on the second Friday of January that they've called it Quitters Day.

Many people make these New Year's resolutions with great intentions. They also have reasonable motivation to achieve their goal, but they still fail to follow through. This failure could be the result of their mentality or environment.

Self-regulation and mindset heavily impact our goal achievement. We're more likely to demonstrate self-regulation when we hold a growth mindset[63].

Self-regulation works alongside our motivation to help us remain focused on learning. Typically driven by intrinsic goals, self-regulation is the source of our desire to learn something new, explore things we don't know, build new skills, and adjust our approach to achieve our goals. When we self-regulate, we choose to pursue new goals. Then, we identify ways to achieve them and track our progress. We're less reliant on others to inspire us with extrinsic rewards, but instead continually try to align to goals we have set for ourselves.

Our mindset works closely alongside our self-regulation. Renowned psychologist and Stanford professor Carol Dweck is a leader in this space, with substantial research behind her work on fixed versus growth mindsets[64].

When we have a fixed mindset, we believe we're born with inherent qualities, like intelligence or talent, which are pre-established and can't change. With this mindset, there's no need to exert effort to achieve a goal. If your talents and abilities are fixed, any increased effort will be in vain. You can't learn or improve anyway, so why try?

With a growth mindset, you know you can improve your intelligence, skills, and talents through dedication and hard work. Highly successful people have a growth mindset, as they constantly try to improve, embracing failure as situational and striving toward ongoing incremental improvements. They proactively identify areas to improve upon and expand on their strengths through deliberate ongoing efforts.

When self-regulation and a growth mindset work together, building on a base of strong motivation, we create the context to achieve our goals. As we work to create psychological safety, our self-regulation influences us to create clear goals for ourselves and our team, track progress, and regularly collect feedback along the way. Our growth mindset embraces failure as part of the process, learns from those experiences, and supports our continued journey to creating a better work environment.

That leads us to the final component, the context in which we are pursuing this new skill.

Environment

Unlike our motivation and mentality that feed self-regulation and mindset, our environment is external to us. So, it might at first feel counterintuitive to include our environment in a conversation about what we control in our personal psychological safety journey. But it's essential to also consider what we can control within our environment.

Our ability to integrate learning is directly impacted by our social and physical environment. Our environment melds with us as individuals to support or reduce our motivation to learn. This environment is an aggregation of our culture and historical diversity, influenced by our families and the broader social constructs in our communities.

We are more likely to maintain motivation and continue learning when we feel we belong and are safe.

This might feel like a Catch-22; psychological safety creates an environment that allows us to learn a new skill, but we need to learn psychological safety before we can create a safe environment. By simply acknowledging this potential tension in our journey we can recognize environmental challenges and begin to explore where to make improvements.

We can focus on the environmental factors where we have high control. At work, we likely have at least some control over our social interactions. We can choose to spend any personal time with those who will support our journey, encourage us to continue when learning becomes difficult, and provide constructive feedback along the way. We can also likely control some of our physical environment. If the office does not initially feel like the best place to practice developing psychological safety, you could take a walk outside or consider testing some ideas with family at home.

The idea isn't necessarily to pick a single path and follow it, but to explore paths, get lost, stumble and continue … knowing each step forward will get you closer to a feeling of safety.

You're Human

If maintaining motivation to self-regulate toward a growth mindset and consciously create a supportive environment weren't difficult enough, we'll add in one more variable. Our brains cannot sustain constant learning. It's important to allow ourselves a break.

Humans have limited energy and capacity to work each day and each of us is a complex mixture of behavior and emotion, skill and will. We might demonstrate open communication and receptivity to feedback in some moments but feel more closed and less receptive in others. In other words, our ability to be open—to demonstrate and receive psychological safety—will fluctuate throughout the day, and on different days. All of this is normal.

This variability in mental energy is related to a limitation in what Nobel Prize winner and notable psychologist Daniel Kahneman calls System 2 Thinking[65]. System 2 describes the moments when we're using the prefrontal cortex of our brain to think deliberately, often associated with slower, calculated, and conscious thoughts. We use this part of our brain when we try to solve a math problem, focus on the perfect wording to the email we're writing, and when we learn a new skill. For each of these detailed tasks, we must remain focused if we're going to successfully complete them. We could call this effort our "controlled behavior."

Kahneman also describes System 1 Thinking, which we use in the moments when we act with less consciousness and with more intuitive or automatic actions. The amygdala hijack, the phenomenon we reviewed earlier that supports our fight-or-flight response to stressful situations, is part of our System 1 thinking. Our brain doesn't wait for us to analyze the situation when we encounter a leopard. Our brains and bodies process the information almost instantaneously so we can survive. System 1 accounts for much of our daily mental activity, including the many routines we complete mindlessly, like brushing our teeth. We could also call this our "automatic behavior."

My son currently uses his controlled thinking to brush his teeth, but with deliberate effort and concentration over time his behavior will become more automatic. This is when the skill becomes a habit.

We're limited in how much time and energy we can successfully dedicate to controlled thinking throughout the day. Just like our body needs rest after a difficult workout, our ability to control our mental effort wanes after a mental challenge. This is why we need breaks from studying for exams or might feel more agitated and less patient at the end of a long workday. Our brains and bodies are signaling to us that we've spent a lot of deliberate mental energy focused on learning, problem solving, and delivering work to achieve deadlines. We have reached our limit of productive work.

Each of us has a limit to how much effort we can give to controlled processing. But like an athlete who trains to improve performance, we can increase our ability to sustain mental effort with practice.

This brings us back to the difficulty we might feel as we pursue psychological safety for ourselves and others, as it is all part of the journey. When we combine our positive motivation with our mentality and environment we can move forward through the challenge. It's natural to expect and therefore be mentally prepared for moments of tiredness and frustration.

I invite you to treat yourself with grace and patience as you move forward. I've seen firsthand the value of sticking to this journey.

In a psychologically safe environment, everyone embraces the growth mindset and openly discusses failures and successes with the desire to continually improve … and without judgment. With a growth mindset, each of us can be confident speaking up, sharing ideas, and challenging others in a positive way. We can embrace failure to learn and grow, instead of avoiding failure due to fear. The value we gain from this is naturally intrinsic, since it helps us to feel safe and respected at work, while also supporting our extrinsic business and career goals.

What challenging activities do you pursue for fun, independent of the outcome? How can you achieve that same level of motivation in the pursuit of psychological safety? Consider your purpose, autonomy, and desire for mastery.

What activities and outcomes will you consider as you define psychological safety goals for yourself? For your team? For your organization?

In what environment do you feel the most freedom to speak your mind and share ideas? How can you begin to replicate that environment at work?

How can you recognize when you need a mental break? What type of break can help you feel most rejuvenated?

CHAPTER 5:
EMBRACE THE LEARNING JOURNEY

On March 11, 2020, the World Health Organization (WHO) declared the first worldwide pandemic[66] since the 1960s[67]. COVID-19 has since reached the unfortunate scale to be in the top-ten deadliest pandemics in human history[68], causing significant increases in depression and anxiety[69]. This depression and anxiety disproportionately impacted people in locations highly impacted by COVID-19, particularly women and people in their early 20s.

To help support mental health improvements, the World Health Organization (WHO) and others recommended finding a hobby that reduced screen time and created space to pursue activities we enjoy[70] [71]. So, it's not surprising six in ten Americans began a new hobby during the years of the COVID-19 pandemic[72].

Learning guitar was among the most popular of these new hobbies, with 16 million people deciding to learn how to play during the pandemic[73]. In a survey of more than 10,000 new and aspiring guitarists, guitar maker Fender found that most respondents wanted to learn a new skill so they could play solo or in front of close friends or family. They were not trying to become a famous paid musician.

New guitar players were interested in improving themselves, not impressing others. In other words, they were motivated intrinsically. And half of all new guitarists are women. The old stereotype of guitarists as a boy's club is finally going away.

We'll consider Gabriella, a 25-year-old woman whose playing is reflected in the Fender survey. She was feeling isolated during the global pandemic and craved a mental release from the monotony of time alone at home. After picking up a few books, baking more cookies than she could eat, and tending a garden outside she decided it was time to build a new skill. And she wanted to meet up with others when COVID-19 allowed.

Gabriella had never played an instrument but always aspired to share Sister Rosetta Tharpe's soulful tunes with more people. Known as The Godmother of Rock 'n' Roll, Tharpe started playing guitar at four years old, toured with her mother to sing at churches, and continued playing into adulthood. A Black and queer woman, she pioneered modern rock 'n' roll in the face of prejudice, during the intense time of sexism, segregation, and racism. Tharpe combined the sounds of church and nightclubs into songs that appealed to the masses and directly influenced early rock 'n' roll musicians like Johnny Cash and Elvis Presley. She collaborated with Duke Ellington and joined the famous New York City Cotton Club Revue at age 23[74].

Every time Tharpe's electric guitar and gospel lyrics flowed through the speakers, Gabriella's foot started to bounce to the beat. Perhaps it was Tharpe's contagious energy, inspiring voice, or spirited guitar playing, but Gabriella knew she wanted to replicate it. She wanted to add her own twist to the sound though, so instead of an electric guitar,

Gabriella picked up an acoustic guitar from her local music shop and signed up for group lessons.

The conditions for Gabriella to learn to play Tharpe's songs on the guitar appear to be aligned with what she needed to be successful. The pandemic provided an external stimulus to provide the initial motivation to learn a new skill. She could combine this with her intrinsic motivation to maintain her well-being. She also felt happy and excited to set a goal to play the music of one of her favorite artists. Gabriella was aware that learning to play the guitar like Tharpe would be difficult, but she had a growth mindset and was ready to work through the challenges. And finally, she'd try to create the right environment. She would balance solo practice time, group lessons with a guitar instructor and, if all went well, a performance for her friends.

She was ready to go through the process of learning the new skill. Throughout the learning journey, Gabriella would experience a range of emotions.

Process

As we've covered, most new skills require deliberate effort to learn. We must start without knowing what we're doing, try, collect feedback, adjust our approach, try again, and repeat until we reach the desired skill level. This process of learning requires a combination of skill development and emotional awareness.

Education and consulting industries have developed a plethora of complex frameworks and taxonomies to try to explain how we learn. Each is valuable but each is also lacking because it is difficult (perhaps impossible) to capture all that we feel and experience during a learning process. We experience the world differently from each other, so even if one of the approaches fully describes how you feel about learning, it likely will miss some key components of what I experience.

I have reviewed more than a dozen of these learning process models and worked closely with a few of them. Most consider how we develop across four stages, starting with the absence of knowledge and transitioning with practice to a state of flow, in which the effort to perform the skill becomes minimal.

We start this process by Anticipating. This can show up as anxiety because we don't know what is to come, or as excitement about the journey. At this point, we don't know what we don't know. After we begin the process, we become Aware of the challenge ahead. We can now more appropriately assess our ability versus what we hope to achieve. After we practice over time and collect feedback to improve, we will become Adept, but we still have to exert mental energy to demonstrate the skill. Finally, after significant repeated effort, we can hope to reach a level of skill understanding that puts us into a flow. We can describe this flow as Automatic, where we no longer need to think about the skill when we do it.

ANTICIPATING	AWARE	ADEPT	AUTOMATIC
You don't know what you need to do, nor how to do it.	You know what you need to do, but are unable to do it.	You are able to do what you need to do, but it still requires deliberate effort.	You can do what you need to do with minimal effort, as an unconscious habit.

Figure 4: When we learn a new skill, most of us progress from a state of anticipating toward an ability to demonstrate the skill with little thought.

Gabriella could follow a simplified learning journey similar to this.

Anticipating: Gabriella's energy is high. She walks into her first lesson with an excitement she hasn't felt in a while and with images of her favorite Tharpe songs flowing from the strings. Although she realizes it's unlikely, she hopes to be able to start playing a song by the end of her first lesson. At this moment, Gabriella does not know the effort required to learn guitar, what skills she'll need to develop, nor how to develop them.

Aware: Gabriella sits in a classroom with other new guitarists and across from her instructor. He asks each of them to set the guitar down. They aren't going to play any music during the first lesson. Gabriella reluctantly sets the guitar beside her, as the instructor begins to teach them some of the basics. Before she starts to play, she will learn the names for the many parts of the guitar and will begin to study the tuning of each string, chord diagrams and the associated guitar chords. Only then can she pick up the guitar and start beginner finger exercises, which will help her build dexterity and map the finger placement to the chords. She won't actually play any music yet, though. Gabriella now realizes she's not going to be strumming melodies at home or entertaining her friends anytime soon. She has a lot to learn before she'll be ready to perform a song. This learning will tap into Gabriella's controlled thinking that we discussed above, requiring significant mental energy to develop her new skill.

Adept: After a few months of daily practice, Gabriella knows all the names for the guitar parts and can play some songs well, but she still must dedicate a lot of mental energy to place her fingers on the right chords and match them to the sounds she wants to produce.

Automatic: Fast forward a couple years, with Gabriella continuing to practice daily and perform songs for friends at parties. She can pick up the guitar, place her fingers on the right chords, and play a song without thinking. Playing the guitar has become a habit, and Gabriella has transitioned from controlled thinking to automatic. She can perform with little exertion of mental energy. She would make Tharpe proud!

In this simplified example, Gabriella's learning process was linear. In real life our anticipation, awareness, and adeptness become intertwined and overlap. For example, Gabriella might have grasped the music language and naming for the guitar parts easily, allowing her to jump from Anticipating to Adept for that part of the learning journey. But learning all the guitar chords and developing the skills to play them adeptly would likely be more challenging. She could have moments of feeling Adept in one practice session, where she's able to easily play a less technical song, followed by other sessions where she feels Aware of her inability while trying the same chords on a more technical song. It's normal for us to bounce around and between these levels of learning as we continue to grow.

Each of us will experience a similar journey as we pursue psychological safety for ourselves and others. Creating the right environment for psychological safety is a skill that requires ongoing attention and adjustment, based on the needs of our current situation. Just as Gabriella would regularly transition between phases while learning to play the guitar, each of us will also need to continually iterate to achieve psychological safety. We might begin with feelings aligned to Anticipating, shift to being more Aware as we start the process, build our skills to the point where we are Adept at creating psychologically safe spaces, and hopefully achieve a level of skill that makes our relative efforts Automatic.

Feelings

As with anyone learning something new, Gabriella will feel a range of emotions as she goes through this learning process. She might experience the bystander effect, diffusion of responsibility, emotional contagion, and imposter syndrome[75]. We all experience similar feelings during our journey toward psychological safety. Each feeling could hold us back from achieving our goals if we're not aware of how it's impacting us. But if we acknowledge these common feelings and discuss them when they show up, we can identify productive ways to work through them.

By knowing we need to look out for these potential challenges we are better equipped to avoid their pitfalls.

After the first few months of instruction, Gabriella and each of the students in her group guitar lesson have learned enough to play some partial songs. They just need to practice, get feedback, and continue to build their skills. At this point, the instructor introduces a new approach to the class.

Near the end of each session the instructor asks the students to practice 60 seconds of guitar in front of the room. At the end of their practice he asks the other students to provide feedback. What went well? What could they improve upon? This querying helps the practicing student get comfortable making mistakes in front of an audience. It also helps the rest of the class continue to refine their ability to identify successful guitar playing as well as elements that need improvement. Most of the students enjoy the practice, but it requires significant controlled effort as they know they still have a lot to learn and will be critiqued.

Gabriella often remains silent during this part of class. She feels uncomfortable critiquing another student's performance or offering ideas for improvement, although each of them craves the feedback. They did, after all, sign up for the instruction in order to play better.

She also notices that the other students tend to remain silent when it's time for them to share feedback. Most look around the room to see what others are doing. Some glance downward to avoid eye contact because they don't want to be called upon. They remain silent, even when they have ideas to share.

In these moments, Gabriella and her classmates could be feeling the "bystander effect" and "diffusion of responsibility." Popularized by social psychologists Bibb Latané and John Darley in their 1964 study[76], the bystander effect describes the tendency for each of us to take less action when we are in a group versus being alone. The likelihood for each of us to speak up decreases even further if the other members of the group are also passive. Phrased differently, we're more likely to take action when alone than when we're in a group, and in group situations we're more likely to become a bystander, not taking action. Most of these studies consider our actions during a time of crisis or potential danger, but we can unintentionally also remain bystanders in other situations, like a guitar lesson or team meeting.

Latané and Darley also explored diffusion of responsibility, a phenomenon that overlaps with the bystander effect but remains differentiated. In their 1968 study[77] they found that people are slower and less likely to report someone in distress to the authorities when in the presence of others. When asked about their lack of response, participants described their competing desire of wanting to help, but also not wanting to "make fools" of themselves by overreacting when others were not reacting. That desire to align to the group response resulted in the lack of action, even when they could speak up to help someone.

While giving feedback on a 60 second guitar practice isn't as severe as reporting someone in physical distress, the feeling can be similar. We often mimic the actions (or inactions) of people around us. If we are aware of this common response phenomenon, we can deliberately make a different choice. Instead of remaining silent when someone asks for feedback, we can provide our productive feedback. This might even inspire others to follow your lead and share their ideas.

Gabriella is feeling extra confident in one of the practice sessions. She's been practicing her favorite Tharpe song, *Strange Things Happening Every Day*, and she's ready to perform.

For the first time since the instructor started having them practice, Gabriella eagerly anticipates sharing what she has learned. She wears her favorite dress and approaches the front of the class with a bounce to her step. Instead of sitting, as most of the students have done before her, she stands confidently and begins to strum the strings. A smile spreads across her face and a surge of adrenaline rushes through her. The sound coming from her guitar is a near replica of *Strange Things Happening Every Day*!

She is thrilled all the practice is finally paying off.

Everyone in the class feels her positive energy and the smiles begin to spread across their faces. They all stand to cheer when Gabriella is done. It feels like Gabriella's positive energy is flowing through the room, infecting everyone around her. This is known as "emotional contagion."

Emotions are like a cold or flu, often accidentally and unknowingly transferring to those around us. Scientists first published studies about this idea of emotional contagion in the early 1990s[78] when they found that we often unconsciously mimic others' behavior and movements. As we mimic behavior we also can catch their emotions, similar to how we'd catch a contagious illness.

If I'm sitting across a table from you and see you scratch your chin during a moment of reflection, I'll likely also touch my face. Neither of us would be aware of my behavior mimicking, until it became top of mind from reading this sentence. It happens involuntarily and automatically. This mimicking behavior starts as early as our infancy[79] and for the most part, creates a positive social connection between us[80].

Gabriella's classmates are all thrilled with her progress and the room is filled with positive vibes. Then it's time for her classmate Pablo to perform. Gabriella returns to her seat after receiving some feedback and Pablo walks to the front of the room. As he takes a seat and picks up his guitar, a rush of stage-fright surges through him.

The joy he just felt shifts to nervousness. His hands shake as he makes final adjustments to his strings, trying to delay his practice because he's suddenly unable to remember the beginning of the song he planned to perform. Pablo is now thinking about how Gabriella has become a great guitarist, and how he could never be as good as her.

Doubt starts flowing through his mind and Pablo questions if he should even bother taking more guitar lessons. He has learned a few simpler songs, but nothing as good as Gabriella. Maybe he should just give up since he's not learning as quickly as his classmate.

Pablo is feeling "imposter syndrome."

Originally termed "imposter phenomenon" by psychologists Pauline Clance and Suzanne Imes in 1978[81], imposter syndrome is when an individual doubts their abilities and accomplishments despite any objective and outstanding accomplishments they've achieved. This can make us fear being exposed as a fraud, particularly if we're compared to our peers.

As many as eight in ten of us have experienced imposter syndrome, with it impacting ethnic minority groups more than others[82]. Pablo is not alone in this feeling. If he shared his feelings with his classmates, he would find that most of them have similar fears.

We are not alone when we follow the actions of a group, take on the feelings of those around us, and feel we might not be good enough.

There is power in recognizing these feelings. When we understand what is happening to and within us we can name it, share our feelings with others, and consider ways to create more positive experiences for all of us. This is exactly what we're trying to achieve with psychological safety. We want to create spaces for open dialogue without fear of repercussion. This knowledge empowers us to start the conversation. Knowing these four feelings—bystander effect, diffusion of responsibility, emotional contagion, and imposter syndrome—allows us to proactively support ourselves and others through our growth journey, since we'll likely have doubts and fears along the way.

Starting the conversation might feel difficult though, since many of us do not enjoy sharing our feelings with others, especially at work. Each of us has different predispositions toward sharing our feelings. So, we will now explore an analogy to help us recognize our and other's interest in these discussions, supporting our shared ability to begin the conversation.

At what point on the psychological safety learning journey are you? At what point are your teammates?

In what group situations do you hold back your ideas, even when you know those ideas could help someone or improve a business outcome? How can you create the conditions to allow for speaking up next time?

Imagine the last time someone else's happiness made you happy. How can you replicate that feeling at work? How can you recognize and address when negativity from others is bringing you down?

In what situations do you feel like you are not good enough? What are three things you do well in those situations?

Sharing

Gabriella continues to practice in her group guitar lesson to learn to play more of Tharpe's songs. She and others show up at the lessons to learn guitar, but they don't spend any time talking about why they are there. They don't share their thoughts or feelings about music, or any of their deep-rooted attitudes or values that brought them there.

Gabriella's time in class is transactional. She shows up, exchanges brief greetings, learns the lesson of the day, practices, gets feedback, and goes home.

This might feel like many of our experiences at work. We can show up, know just enough about our coworkers to get the job done, and then go home. At work and with people with whom we don't have a deep or close relationship, others are most likely only aware of our behaviors and not our internal processing. They can see what we do, but don't understand why we do it. But much of our behavior is dictated by our feelings, thoughts, attitudes, and values. In some cases, we aren't even aware of how these feelings and attitudes influence what we do. We simply perform our work duties and go home.

This approach to work is very reasonable in many work environments where busy and hectic schedules aligned to achieving difficult goals make it challenging to stop and learn more about each other. In work environments with low psychological safety we are even more likely to hold back our feelings and thoughts for fear of others judging us. We often focus on simply getting the work done with little understanding of what drives that behavior.

What if we were comfortable sharing more, though? How could that sharing help to build empathy and invite discussions, instead of judgment and assumptions? We could start to build human connections and support ongoing growth aligned to individual and team needs, instead of to misinformed criticism. We are more likely to embrace these conversations when we recognize how we relate to similar emotions (like those described above), and maybe even life experiences.

Much of what we see from others, and what we show to others, is driven by powerful invisible forces. Our values are influenced by our cultural identity, education, political affiliation, family structure and economic circumstances. These values impact our attitudes, feelings, and thoughts, all culminating in what manifests in our behaviors. But in many cases at work, we know nothing about our coworkers' values, attitudes, feelings, and thoughts beyond cursory conversations and brief reflections of attitudes.

We are a lot like Aspen trees.

One Aspen grove in Utah is among the oldest and largest organisms in the world, estimated to be 14,000 years old, covering 106 acres and weighing 13 million pounds[83]! The untrained hiker would walk through this massive grove of trees and believe they are seeing thousands of single trees, but a grove of Aspens is actually one plant with a shared system of roots. Much of the Aspen's life is hidden, as it pulls carbon dioxide from the air to produce food that allows it to grow, along with water and nutrients from its roots underground. A 150-year-old mature Aspen growth could sit alongside a young sapling of less than a year, sharing a single root-system, essentially drinking from the same straw into the ground. When the old tree dies, another sprouts in its place in a constant cycle of regeneration, growth, and death. All this birth and death occurs within a single Aspen plant.

Much of what we see of the Aspen above ground is the result of invisible forces of air and roots, just like much of the behavior we see in our coworkers is the result of what they have experienced in their lives, been taught, or felt. Each of us might feel strong and proud, standing tall like a mature Aspen growth in moments of confidence. And we can simultaneously feel uncertain or insecure like the struggling sapling, if in a different situation. We remain the same person, with the same roots of experience, but we can show up differently in different situations. Most of these situations do not define us but are opportunities to learn and share with others.

Humans also sprout new interests and learn, try, succeed, fail, fall, and stand again ... supported by the roots of our lives. We choose which parts of our roots, if any, we share with others.

Figure 5: We are like Aspen trees with their beautiful outgrowths enabled by invisible factors of carbon dioxide from the air, and water and nutrients from the ground. Our behaviors, what we show to others, are the direct result of the invisible factors of our values, attitudes, feelings, and thoughts.

Our Aspens bring us back to Gabriella.

With months of practice, Gabriella is finally ready to move beyond her class and perform a few songs in front of ten of her closest friends. She decorates her yard with lights and tables and chairs that face a small stage. She sets out nostalgic memorabilia that creates the mood from the time of Sister Rosetta Tharpe, including pictures of Tharpe's favorite venues and performances. Gabriella starts her Tharpe playlist on her stereo speakers. As the music plays and guests arrive, she begins to feel sentimental. This is Gabriella's first time gathering with all of her friends since the COVID-19 lockdowns started, and it is also the first time any of her friends will hear her play the guitar.

After everyone arrives, greeted with a big hug and smile by Gabriella, they gather around the tables and look toward the stage. She's ready to share her music and invites everyone to sit. Before she plays, she pauses to take in the scene in front of her.

After more than a year of mostly isolation, Gabriella is with her friends. A light breeze causes the lights overhead to sway slightly, as she closes her eyes and takes in a slow deep breath. The air smells a little fresher, with recent spring flowers blooming in the surrounding yards. Dusk is slowly taking over the stage, and Gabriella can almost not believe she's about to perform in front of her friends.

She sits down, picks up her guitar … and starts to cry.

Gabriella's emotions wash over her and come to the surface. She takes this moment to share her thoughts and feelings with her friends in a way she never shared with her guitar classmates. She shares how she was starting to feel depressed because of COVID-19 and needed a new hobby that challenged her and gave her an opportunity to connect with others. That's why she decided to take up the guitar. She then shares her love for Tharpe's music and how she feels inspired by Tharpe's ability to live a life aligned to her passions, overcoming societal expectations of Black queer women. Gabriella feels proud to share Tharpe's music with others and to demonstrate her new guitar skills, and she's thrilled to be able to do this with her best friends. Her friends are drawn into Gabriella's story, empathizing with her experience and appearing to almost feel how she feels. They are fully present and are drawn closer to Gabriella than before.

Gabriella has started to share her roots and by so doing, immediately created a deeper connection with those around her.

In our deeper relationships, including those with close friends and family, our feelings of psychological safety increase because we believe we can share without fear. We expose our roots because we are often more comfortable revealing more about ourselves. These discussions with friends can feel very cathartic, helping us express our emotions in a way we wouldn't otherwise feel comfortable.

If we can bring these feelings of psychological safety to our work teams, we can realize similar benefits. This isn't to say we all have to be friends with coworkers. But as we now know, we are more likely to be successful as individuals, a team, and as a company if we create safety within our work environments to openly share feedback and ideas for improvement.

Since these conversations about feelings, attitudes, and values often don't occur naturally at work, the manager can play a key role here. She can bring the team together in an environment that helps everyone feel more comfortable sharing. She can also provide an analogy like the Aspen to enable and help guide the discussion.

Sharing is not something to force, but to foster and encourage through alignment with our goals. As we show more of our roots, sharing more about what influences our behavior, we're more likely to create the conditions for interpersonal connections[84]. These connections help to build psychological safety since we're more likely to communicate openly when we know those around us care about our well-being and lifegoals, not just the actions we take to complete our work. These improved connections help to make each of us happier and support better team performance that improves our company's business results.

We've now considered how to build psychological safety for ourselves. We recognize we have the most control over what we do and how we respond to situations. We understand the power of our motivation, mentality, and environment for learning a new skill. We might not always want to share how we feel about things, but when given the opportunity, we recognize how we can create connections with others through sharing. We are not alone in any of this, as most of us have similar experiences when we learn a new skill.

Now that we've reflected on how we might experience this journey toward psychological safety as individuals, we're better prepared to think about how we can bring psychological safety to those around us. We are ready to explore how to build psychological safety across our team.

What thoughts, feelings, attitudes, and values are you comfortable sharing?

What holds you back from sharing more?

PART THREE:

Team Integration—

Support Psychological Safety Within the Team

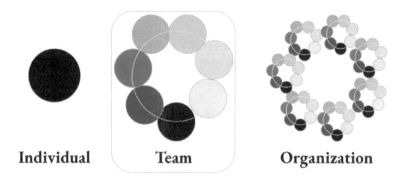

Individual   **Team**   **Organization**

We have the most control over our personal feelings of psychological safety, but we have more impact when we can expand that safety to those with whom we work. This is our opportunity to transcend individual barriers and create connections between team members that support better outcomes for each of us.

We started by considering what we can control, focusing on our personal reflection and understanding of psychological safety. We will now consider how we can share what we have learned and support others. We cannot control how psychologically safe others feel, but we can support the working environment and personal connections that inspire others to pursue this safety.

In this section we'll explore others' perspectives and continue to build comfort sharing ours. We'll connect psychological safety to one of the most important business processes we all likely experience: setting clear goals and aligning the team to achieve those goals. We'll consider how the journey we might experience as a team is similar to how we follow an individual learning journey. Finally, we'll review opportunities for ongoing discussions. These discussions, which create dedicated space for sharing ideas, are crucial for enabling psychological safety to thrive.

Dr. Amy Edmondson, the Harvard Business School Professor and leader in psychological safety, focuses her research on teams because nearly all work we do requires working with others[85]. Edmondson explains that psychological safety lives at the group level, shaped by team leads and local leaders. I experienced this throughout my time at Google where some teams felt significant psychological safety, with members sharing ideas and bringing their full selves to work. These teams tended to show continuous growth and improvement, sustaining long-term target achievement through collaborative effort, and quickly adjusting when they failed to achieve targets. They often also helped other teams improve by expanding their positive influence to a larger group.

Unfortunately, other Google teams failed to develop this level of psychological safety, with many individuals afraid to share their perspectives for fear of repercussions from leadership. These teams had higher employee turnover, unhealthy inter-team competition, often suffered from overlapping efforts across teams due to poor communication and were slower to complete their work.

The optimal team size to start building psychological safety is less than ten.

Stanford's Bob Sutton found that we have our most effective meetings when they include five to nine people[86]. This aligns with Harvard's George Miller finding that humans can hold approximately seven things top of mind in any moment[87]. As we expand the size of our team, we lose our ability to focus on what we hope to achieve—building psychological safety and exceeding our goals. Instead of focusing on our goal, we dedicate effort to supporting interpersonal relationships and group logistics.

No need to worry if you work on a larger or smaller team! I've successfully built psychological safety in the teams I've directly managed, with team sizes from two to more than twenty people. But I have found we often could have richer and more open discussions earlier in the process when the team had five to ten people. From there we could then expand what we'd learned and developed into the broader organization. It's possible to take what you learn here to a team of any size.

Much of what you'll learn in this section will be phrased in terms of what a leader can do with her teams, but the information is also applicable when you are not the manager. Each team member can inspire their manager or lead sessions themselves. One fun place to start can be with stories.

 In what team environment have you felt most psychologically safe? What about that team helped to create those feelings of safety?

CHAPTER 6:
SHARE STORIES

About a year ago a friend recommended a new show I should watch with my kids, ages two and five. When I first heard of *Bluey*, a cartoon about a Blue Heeler puppy and her family, I was skeptical. I'd already encountered too many cartoons made for young children that were sometimes unbearable to sit through. I didn't want to add another to our list of shows the kids requested and I reluctantly agreed to watch.

I quickly learned that *Bluey* was not your normal kid's cartoon. I was hooked after the first episode I watched, "Baby Race."

I enjoyed "Baby Race" so much that I shared it with my parents and sister. We sat down to watch it, with the adults focused on the cartoon and the kids playing elsewhere. I warned my mom and sister they needed to pay attention to the full episode, particularly the very end. We all sat and focused.

Within a couple minutes, I heard laughter. I looked around to see smiling faces. In this episode, baby Bluey was learning to sit, crawl, and walk. She didn't take the traditional approach. Instead of crawling forward, she rolled to get across the room, slid on her bum, and crawled backward like a lobster. It was hilarious.

The mood then shifted to somberness. Bluey's mom, Chilli, thought she was a bad mom. She felt she was doing something wrong, causing Bluey's failure to learn to crawl forward like the other puppies her same age. She took Bluey to the doctor to get checked and tried to show her the right way of moving, but nothing worked. She finally broke down and cried when talking with a friend. The friend shared that Chilli was a great mom and that Bluey would walk when the time was right for her. This lifted the pressure from Chilli.

After deciding to let Bluey follow her own journey, Chilli provided support and love, but no longer pressured her. In the final scene, Chilli is washing dishes in the kitchen when she hears something behind her. She turns to see Bluey walking toward her, arms outreached to give her a hug.

Cue the tears.

The same adults that laughed out loud at the beginning of the episode and watched solemnly through the middle, started to cry (yes, actual tears) at the end.

"Baby Race" is one of at least 130 episodes released in the last five years. The first episode aired in Australia and has since become a worldwide hit, drawing a lot of media attention. I'm glad I listened to my friend's recommendation.

Joe Brumm created *Bluey* to appeal to kids and adults so they can laugh together, not simply tolerate a shared viewing. And he's done something right! *Bluey* has won 15 awards, including a Rockie Award from the BANFF World Media Festival, Critics Choice Awards, and an International Emmy[88]. It's Australia's most streamed show[89] and can be viewed in more than 60 countries[90]. In addition to children and parents, many of *Bluey*'s fans are childless adults[91].

As a result of *Bluey*'s success, Brumm has been interviewed by several top news outlets and has shared his perspectives on many podcasts. He's kindly shared how he created *Bluey* and his approach to writing each episode. Of the many recommendations provided by Brumm to tell a great story, one appears to be consistent across conversations. He starts with his personal experiences. He then crafts a short story that often shows the puppy Bluey working through a challenge. Brumm is very deliberate to remove any non-essential details from the story to fit it into the seven minutes allocated for each episode. As Bluey works through the challenge, she develops a new perspective and continues to grow up through toddlerhood[92]. Like for each of us, the challenges in Bluey's life impact how she shows up later. Those experiences create the basis for her roots.

While I don't expect most of us to have the storytelling brilliance of Joe Brumm, we all have the life experience to craft our own stories. We've all faced a challenge that has influenced how we show up today. Each of us has stories to tell. We just have to decide which story is most important and if we are comfortable sharing it.

Stories help bring us together, build empathy, and inspire action. Each of these are important contributors to building psychological safety within teams. When we understand each other's motivations, empathize with each other's experiences, and align to achieve goals in support of each other and the business, we create happier teams that achieve great results.

What stories are you comfortable sharing? Which shaped who you are today?

Build Connections with Stories

When leading teams at Google, the first thing I did with any new team member was share my story and invite theirs. This effort builds on what we considered above; how we can reflect on psychological safety for ourselves. Now that we have considered what parts of our backgrounds have influenced us most and started to think about how our roots influence what we show above ground, we can begin to craft the story we feel comfortable sharing with others.

Sharing includes telling your story and listening to others'.

The simple act of listening to each other's reflections can help to build psychological safety within the group. In a study about inspiring creativity within teams, management consultant Dotan Castro and others found that managers can create increased feelings of psychological safety by listening to their team members[93]. Executive consultant Andrew Fenniman replicated this in his 2010 study, where he found psychological safety to increase for team members with empathic listening by the supervisor[94]. Andrew Kluger and Guy Itzchakov found these benefits to extend to both people in the conversation, sharer and listener, improving their well-being and interpersonal connections[95].

Listening to others can set the stage for psychological safety, and this act of listening is a skill. When we listen well, we aren't distracted by other thoughts, and we aren't trying to interject our opinion. Instead, we're fully engaged and processing what the other person is telling us through their words, tone, and body language. We don't interrupt. We simply focus our energy on the other person, allow them to share, and ask questions when appropriate. During a busy workday, with personal and work distractions pulling your attention elsewhere, it might feel difficult to isolate your focus on someone else, but this effort will pay off for you and your team as you begin to build psychological safety.

Whenever someone new joined my team at Google, and when I took over a new team, I dedicated our first one-to-one conversations to learning about them and sharing about myself. Unless we had something urgent to discuss for work, we postponed any work task discussions until we had a chance to learn more about each other. These conversations were genuine, open, honest, and often vulnerable.

Despite repeating this process more than 150 times over more than a decade, I continued to iterate and tried to adjust to feedback. My goal was always to create a personal connection and comfort early in the relationship, supporting open dialogue with everyone I worked with. My exact approach won't work for everyone, but I hope you'll find pieces that resonate and feel genuine so you can bring something similar to your teams. I've had team members refer to our first conversations more than twelve years after we worked together, sharing that these introductory discussions helped frame our relationships with high psychological safety. For some, these early conversations positively influenced how they approached their careers.

In most cases, the conversation started with the team member sharing. But this sharing felt uncomfortable for some, so I was always happy to share my story first if it helped to model open communication. To help make them comfortable I emailed them questions before our first meeting so they could formulate their thoughts. They could either respond in an email or discuss in our meeting, whichever felt more comfortable to them. My goal was to help each new team member begin to tell their story.

I've shared the list of questions I sent to new team members below. I borrowed and iterated these questions from one of my favorite leaders at Google[96]. I'll always remember his genuine interest in me and I hoped to bring the same positive feeling to others. The team members didn't have to answer all the questions, just those with which they were comfortable. You'll notice each of the questions is written open-ended, starting with "what" or "how." Asking open-ended questions is a deliberate coaching approach to inspire a thoughtful response, which we will explore more later.

- What are your personal goals? What are your professional goals? How can I help you achieve them? (It's alright if you don't know!)
- What are three things you liked about previous managers? What are three things you disliked about previous managers? (If you prefer, you can share thoughts about a teacher or coach instead.)
- What are three things you liked about previous roles at Google? What are three things you disliked about previous roles at Google? (If this is your first role at Google, consider previous experiences.)
- What do you hope to learn from me?
- What do you hope to learn from Google?
- What excites you most about this role?
- What else would you like me to know?

During these discussions, and as I continued to learn more about each person on my team, I took diligent notes, capturing what they shared so I could easily remember and reference the details in the future. By the time I left Google, I had a single Google Sheet with a separate tab for each of more than 100 team members. I could easily refer to current and previous team members to remember their goals, motivations, and impact during our time working together. My process allowed me to more easily create and communicate performance reviews aligned to their goals and, in many cases, write detailed letters of recommendation for prior team members when they searched for new employers. Learning about them helped me support their journey and goals, even when those goals extended beyond my team or Google.

In addition to me learning about the new team member, I also shared my background, management style, leadership philosophy, and values. Like *Bluey's* Joe Brumm, I started with my personal experiences, shared a few life challenges, the steps I took to overcome them, and how those experiences led me to what matters most to me now. I hoped to create a genuine connection with everyone on my team with this brief overview. Unlike Brumm, I don't think I ever inspired belly laughs or tears. My story would often show up as something like this:

I grew up in Cincinnati and have one older sister, who is one of my best friends. We spent a lot of time outside, camping, playing soccer, and exploring local parks. I'm still really close with my family and miss them, even after many years of living away from them. After high school I attended five colleges, starting at Ohio State studying Chemistry, but it just didn't feel like the right fit for me. So, I dropped out and moved back home for almost a year, where I wrote a book about a cycling trip I took from Cincinnati to Jackson Hole, Wyoming between my Freshman and Sophomore years at

Ohio State. I rode 1,900 miles, pulling a trailer packed with my tent and gear, at age 19. Life then took me to Xavier University to study Biology. Between my two semesters at Xavier, I lived in Boulder, Colorado, for a summer and fell in love with it, so I transferred one more time before I completed my BA in Environmental Biology in Boulder. I have a lot of interests, so these changes in college let me experience a lot of different things!

I then moved back to Cincinnati again, where I was a temporary Chemist for Procter & Gamble for six months to study improvements to diaper absorption. I followed that by starting a small clothing company that donated 10% of all profits to charities while completing my masters in Biology at the University of Cincinnati. I applied to more than twenty jobs, with no luck getting an offer because I was always over or under-qualified. I was really frustrated and didn't know what to do, so I decided to get an MBA. I assumed an MBA would actually help me get a job.

That led me to the University of Michigan, my final (as of now) university and degree, and I was lucky to get a job at Google after graduating. Google was the first company to offer me a full-time job with benefits, and I was 29! Most companies I talked with thought I was flakey because of my diverse experiences and background. Luckily Google recognized my path as paved with genuine curiosity with success along the way and saw my potential.

I started in my dream location of Denver, Colorado, and was devastated when the office closed in 2008. That office closing resulted in a very difficult personal relationship breakup and me leaving one of my favorite places in the world. After the office closed, I moved with Google to San Francisco, then Ann Arbor for my first manager role, and then to the Chicago office. I met my wife Colleen (ex-Googler) while I was in Ann Arbor, and we have two kids, Sierra and Jackson, and their furry brother Cooper—our dog.

I have three things that matter most to me in life.

1. *My friends and family are always first, and work is always secondary to them. I'll prioritize the support of great friends and family over most other things, including my career. So, I'm very deliberate with how I spend my time at work and away.*

2. *I have a strong desire to give back to the world, including my relationships within and outside of Google. Since I don't have a lot of extra time while working full time and co-raising a family, this mostly shows up as financial donations, but I hope to dedicate more of my time to supporting philanthropic efforts after I leave Google. Part of why I've stayed at Google for so long is because it affords me the ability to donate money to others, and because I hope my savings will allow me to quit corporate work without having to worry about money, allowing me to also donate my time to others.*

3. *Adventures fuel my energy for everything else I do. These adventures include mountaineering (I have a list of peaks I hope to climb around the world), marathons, triathlons and random exploration. If I fail to take adventures, I struggle to bring my full self and energy to work and family.*

And finally, I'll leave you with my leadership philosophy.

1. *You: I'm a manager because of you. I prioritize you and our team before any of our targets. I lead with love, so I will celebrate your successes and will challenge you to improve, knowing almost everything we do is situational and we can become better over time. I hope you'll do the same with me, celebrating my successes and challenging me when I do things that can improve, of which there will be many. This isn't to say we can always be happy and get the things we want, but to know we're all safe and will move through difficult challenges and growth opportunities together, and with best intentions for our ongoing growth.*

2. *Customers: If we approach our relationship with love and open*

communication, we will be well equipped to support our customers. For a sales or services team, this is an external customer. For an enablement team, our customer is another Googler and their team. Our primary responsibility is to help our customers achieve their goals. This requires us to truly understand their needs and goals, challenge them if we see an opportunity to improve, and then support their success. I've gone so far as to tell a Chief Marketing Officer to spend as much as they can with a competitor that outperformed Google Ads because that better served their goals and objectives. Genuine discussions like this resulted in significant revenue growth for Google while sustaining customer success, because the customer knew we always led with their interests first.

3. *Google: If we communicate openly and with love, followed by helping customers achieve their goals, Google will thrive. Google always comes third because our success is the result of the other things done well, not an action in itself.*

If you'd like to learn more about me and my leadership approach, you can visit my Google Doc any time. I'm here to continue to share and answer questions, as you have them.

I captured my story in a Google Doc and made it available to all Googlers. The document included much of the information from our introductory meeting, along with some additional important context about me. It supported my team members if they ever wanted to learn more about me, and I also shared it with partner groups to support better working relationships beyond my teams.

From the first moment I spent with each member of my team, I was genuine to myself and vulnerable with them. In these conversations I shared my journey, including the failures and difficult moments, along with how I worked through them. Even with my setbacks and uncertainties, I still had a long and successful Google career.

I shared my story in this way because I hoped to begin a personal connection and help team members understand how I approach leadership. By modeling the behavior, I hoped everyone on the team would begin to feel comfortable doing the same. When we achieved this on a team, we all spoke openly, continually improved. and regularly excelled against our business goals.

We all remained very driven, but egos largely disappeared. Our team success all started by telling our stories.

My introductory story took approximately the same time as one *Bluey* episode. There are a few components to this introduction that I've found to be particularly important, based on feedback from my teams-Personal, Predispositions, and Preferences.

Personal

My story included personal information about growing up in my family, a challenging relationship break up, a cycling adventure I took, another book I wrote, and the non-linear path I took to arrive at my career. These details helped to make me who I am and helped the new team member quickly understand me beyond the workplace. I only shared what felt comfortable to me.

I failed many times along my journey. I dropped out of my first college, couldn't find a job after getting my first master's degree, and struggled to find the right approach to my career. It's often easy to look at someone in a leadership position and assume it was always easy for them, particularly when that person is a cisgender, White, upper middle-class, well-educated male. But even with the many privileges I know I experienced, each of us takes a different path and encounters our own difficulties.

I also shared openly about what mattered most to me in life, likely to a fault. I even proactively shared with the senior leadership for each team I was on, so every one of my managers knew my plans to leave Google when the time was right. While I had a very successful career at Google, my sharing undoubtedly inhibited my upward trajectory to executive roles because I was clear my long-term work interest was elsewhere. The honest approach was right for me because it allowed me to genuinely engage in all relationships with the intention that everyone would benefit from the discussion and feel empowered to share their priorities. It also allowed senior leadership to prioritize executive roles for those who wanted to stay at Google longer, which was better for the company.

Predispositions

I took many personality assessments at Google, so I shared the results, including the category name and descriptions. I shared my results for StrengthsFinder[97], Insights Discovery[98], and True Colors[99]. Each assessment supported a better understanding of my natural predispositions and biases. For example, True Colors aligns four different colors to different descriptors about the person's presumed predispositions. I tended to score highly on Orange and Green for True Colors, followed closely by Blue. I scored very low on Gold.

The assessment helped me to communicate my tendency to approach things logically and analytically, preferring to think through challenges alone before a group discussion. I enjoy varied experiences that are adventurous, which can sometimes present me as being impulsive. I care deeply about the people I work with, and I tend to approach my work with enthusiasm and sympathy for others. I'm also happy to question rules and authority.

Each of my traits can be strengths or weaknesses, depending on the situation. They are not good nor bad, but just are.

These assessments don't conclusively define me or anyone else, but they help to start a discussion. I can share where I believe the assessment aligns with how I perceive myself, and where it differs. When able, I enjoy having everyone on the team complete these assessments and then discuss how they feel about their own results. This is a great and low-pressure way to support the discussion of diverse viewpoints and approaches, providing the opportunity to embrace similarities and to celebrate differences.

Since I know I have high comfort questioning rules and authority, I called this out as a potential weakness of mine. There are times when following rules and authority are more important than adhering to what I perceive as logic or creativity. I asked those on my team who had a high respect for authority to help balance me in the times I might err toward too much questioning, and to challenge me if they see me taking a path with which they disagree.

Openly discussing each other's predispositions and opportunities for growth is a great contributor to creating psychological safety. The personality assessments provide language and frameworks to begin those discussions.

Preferences

We can determine our work condition preferences by applying more personal reflection, moving beyond the language of a personality assessment. What moments at work make you most happy and feel alive? When do you feel most productive? What conditions allow you to show your best self?

When I consider these questions, I find that four things continually show up.

- If we're going to brainstorm, I prefer to know the problem before we meet, so I can reflect and think on it in advance. I'm at my best with a balance of alone time and team time.
- I tend to work toward positive outcomes and will rarely get mad. I simply ask for honest, open communication and best intentions. If we communicate openly, particularly when it feels challenging after we make mistakes, we can work toward great outcomes over time. The only thing that tends to make me upset is dishonesty.
- I enjoy learning and solving problems, which often leads me to ask questions and pursue details. I always do this with the best intentions, not necessarily because I disagree. I don't want to micromanage.
- I like variety, so I try to incorporate a mix of detailed and big-picture thinking into my job.

These introductory discussions help to build the base for psychological safety. They introduce open dialogue at the start of the relationship, including personal details, joys and challenges, motivations, vulnerabilities, failures, and future goals. All of this sharing is the starting point of a relationship, intended to model vulnerability and inspire each of us to share. In the nearly 150 times I followed this approach my team members appreciated the discussion and it led to follow up stories from both of us.

But these stories do not resonate with everyone.

Many people prefer to keep work and home separate. I understand and respect that. This is not a time to push them to share something personal, but to listen to their perspective and adjust as appropriate. You can continue to share your story, when appropriate and comfortable, but give the other person the space to consider what feels right for them.

Each of us can approach communication in a way that feels genuine. You might have to delve to find the approach that feels right to you, like Bluey—rolling, bum-sliding, and lobster crawling—on your way toward walking. You might need to let go of the desire to force a conversation or connection, just as Chilli eventually let go of the pressure put on Bluey to crawl normally. But if you are patient with yourself and others and allow the space for practice in a way that feels genuine to you and them, in the end you are likely to eventually find a way to crawl forward together.

What additional questions could you ask your team members to understand their goals and preferences?

What aspects of my storytelling resonated with you? What would you like to repeat for yourself and your team? What would you avoid?

Connect Through Shared Learning

I acknowledge this next idea might not be welcome in all workplaces, but this was one of the most powerful experiences I had as a leader. Through book clubs and group discussions about documentaries, my teams and I created connections in a way we could likely never have achieved through our own stories. Moments from these discussions directly shifted my perspectives at work and in life, supporting my own personal development and fostering the same in others.

We read books and reviewed documentaries with provocative and sensitive content, causing some discomfort in the conversations. This helped us practice sharing dissenting opinions about sensitive topics, making it much easier to then share dissenting opinions about less personally emotional topics, like work. It also supported us getting to know each other's perspectives. These conversations created a closeness we could not have achieved otherwise.

If memory serves me correctly, my first book discussion was about *Lean In*[100], Sheryl Sandberg's invitation to women to take more risks and a seat at the table of work conversations. At the time, many women at Google were reading and discussing the book. I was curious about Sandberg's message, and a young man on my team shared this curiosity. So, Chris and I decided to read the book and discuss it as part of our weekly one-to-one meetings.

From an outsider's perspective, this might have appeared a bit curious. We dedicated a portion of our precious working time to discuss a book that was not directly targeted toward us, and it had no connection to our ad sales goals. But it led to very rich conversations that brought us closer together and helped us show up better at work.

As a Black man only a few years into his growing career, Chris could relate to some of the things Sandberg shared about women at work. In an environment filled with predominantly White teammates and leaders, her encouragement to speak up, share ideas, and take a seat at the table served as a great prompt for him to avoid any potential feelings of imposter syndrome. These were also great reminders for me, both for the moments when I was also holding back ideas or did not feel I should be in a room with leaders, but also to build empathy for what others might feel when they work with me. The conversations helped me to look for opportunities to empower the women and those from underrepresented communities on my teams who might have inadvertently held themselves back from their full potential.

This experience led me to later bring book clubs to my team meetings. I never forced these discussions, but instead ensured everyone was comfortable reading the books we selected and the topics we would discuss. If someone was uncomfortable, we selected a different book, and there were no hard feelings if someone didn't read the chapter for the week. We all had very busy schedules at work and home, and the last thing we needed was pressure to dedicate more time to an optional work-related activity.

To my pleasant surprise, nearly everyone participated every week. I acknowledge, despite all efforts, some might have felt compelled by social pressure from the team or assumed unspoken expectations by me, but I believe everyone was genuinely interested in the discussions.

Some of our more intense discussions revolved around *The New Jim Crow*[101]. In the book the author Michelle Alexander, a civil rights lawyer and legal scholar, highlights how the criminalization of African Americans has relegated them to second-class status in the United States. Despite the Civil Rights reforms of the 1960s, African Americans continue to be disproportionately penalized through the War on Drugs. Even with similar drug use across races, Black people are 13.4 times more likely to be sent to state prison than Whites for drug offenses. In some states, Black people make up 90 percent of drug prisoners, despite there being five times as many White people in the United States[102]. This disproportion is driven by racial targeting.

At the time we discussed *The New Jim Crow*, my team was one of the most diverse of my career. It was also small enough to create a safety that could have been challenging to achieve in a larger group. Our team consisted of a Black gay woman, a Jewish woman, a Jewish man, and a woman and a man of Indian descent. I was the only person in the room who could not identify—and hence, fully relate—with a non-dominant US culture or race.

The conversations were rich and open, often diverging from the book content but aligned with the intent. At one point, we were discussing the challenge of building professional networks. The Black gay woman on my team shared that she learned at an early age that she had to proactively build relationships if she wanted to be successful. Looking back, my response was very naive. I shared my long-held feelings about networking; that I tend to feel networking can be disingenuous, so avoid networking opportunities in favor of just believing I'll meet the right people when the time is right.

Her response was direct, honest, and has stuck with me: "That's because you're White."

I immediately felt challenged and maybe a little offended. I thought I was an empathetic leader with an open mind, but I didn't know how to respond to her directness. I can't remember what I said in that moment, but I know my heart was racing a little and my brain was searching for a way to understand the comment.

It wasn't until at least a month later, as I was falling asleep one night, that it hit me. I fully understood. Because I am White and felt the associated privileges my whole life, I was able to ignore networking and still succeed professionally. While not all White people have this same privilege of professional success, as a White man, I'm more likely to already have access to a network that can support my growth and development from a young age. My team member's short comment was inspired by our book club and resulted in an epiphany about my unintentional bias that will stick with me for the rest of my life. We will discuss our networks further, along with research that supports her comment, when we consider how we can support psychological safety across our organization.

That team also discussed Trevor Noah's *Born a Crime*[103] to expand our consideration of race outside of the United States. On another team, we focused more on our behavior and how to influence others with *The Power of Habit*[104]. And on another team, each of us watched the documentary, *13th*[105] and again discussed the disproportionate number of African Americans in the prison system. Each discussion helped to bring our team closer, understand each other's perspectives, and practice how to considerately disagree with each other. We all benefited from new perspectives and the ability to bring what we learned to our work relationships, where we increasingly felt comfortable disagreeing with each other and discussing alternatives.

Consider what type of book club you could have with your team at work.

Invite: What topic could challenge your team enough to inspire difficult conversations, while maintaining enough comfort to gain full engagement?

Share: In what context and location would you and your team feel empowered to have these discussions?

Listen: What conditions can you create to ensure everyone is heard and understood?

Build Empathy with Analogies

As we saw from the book club conversations, storytelling can transcend our personal experiences and invite new ways of thinking.

Analogies can provide a similar benefit, often with a lighter tone to the conversation.

When we empathize with others we have the ability to understand and share their feelings, increasing our feeling of connection with them. This connection can support more open dialogue and sharing, which directly aligns with the development of psychological safety. One way to foster empathy is by taking on others' perspectives, which helps us consider alternative approaches beyond our personal biases.

Since our empathy can be inhibited when we're time constrained or focused on achieving a goal[106], we'll explore two simple analogies to consider others' perspectives in a moment of high stress. Both are intended to provide an easy visual to recall when we feel unintentional judgment or closed-mindedness. We will start with a banana and end with an elephant. Both might prompt you to recall our discussion of the Old Woman/Young Woman image in Chapter 3. All help us to recognize our biases.

The Right Way to Peel a Banana

What if you had a banana and were asked to open it to reveal the fruit inside? What would you do?

According to Chiquita, one of the world leaders in banana distribution, most of us peel the banana from the stem[107]. While I haven't tracked the results of these discussions across my teams, I

suspect nearly nine in ten of my team members also say they would open a banana by the stem. It's like a handle inviting us to pull it! This way of opening the banana can be difficult though, particularly when the banana is ripe and smooshes into itself, instead of peeling away from the fruit.

If you or someone on your team has already researched this, you might have learned the correct way to open a banana.

Pinch here

Instead of pulling the stem, you can pinch the brown tip opposite the stem. With a gentle pinch, the banana peel splits apart, allowing you to easily access the fruit inside, even when the banana is ripe and difficult to open from the stem. A quick Google search will reinforce this is the correct method to open a banana, but what about the other options?

You could cut the banana in half with a knife, snap it in half with your hands, twist it to separate the peel seams, or if you've ever seen a baby attempt this, simply smash it until the fruit oozes out. If you're part of the majority of readers, you started this section with a clear idea of your way to open a banana; the way you've always done it. Then we learned the so-called correct way—easily with a pinch on the brown tip of the banana. But with further reflection, we realize there are many additional ways to get to the fruit.

So, which of these is the right way? None of them! There is no one "correct" approach.

Each of us has our own preference, and each of these approaches gives us access to the fruit. So, the next time you're in a meeting or brainstorming session on a business challenge and you feel adamant your approach is correct and want to convince others to go along with you, think of the banana. In an environment of high psychological safety aligned to common goals, we care less about winning an argument or having the right idea. It's more important to achieve the best outcome for the business and working group.

Psychological safety allows for the sharing of ideas and empowers individuals to let go of the desire to win, in favor of the group's success.

Instead of arguing to win your perspective, ask questions to learn more and empathize with the others' perspectives within your working group. Perhaps you're trying to open the banana from the stem while they want to pinch the opposite end. Their perspective could possibly help you achieve the same shared goal, but with less effort or mess.

Blind Men and an Elephant

The blind men and an elephant is another analogy to help remind us about the limitations of our perspectives and to invite others' ideas. This parable likely arises from India, with early versions found in Buddhist, Hindu, and Jain writing[108]. Six blind men stand around an elephant and reach out to touch it. Having never seen an elephant, each blind man only has the perspective of what their hand feels.

- The first man feels the elephant's side and tells the others an elephant is like a wall.
- The second feels the elephant's smooth and sharp tusk and says an elephant is more like a spear.
- The third blind man touches the elephant's trunk and declares the first two men wrong, since an elephant is like a snake.
- The fourth feels the elephant's leg and describes the elephant as a tree.
- The fifth blind man reaches high and touches the elephant's ear, so he declares the elephant to be like a fan.

- The sixth grabs the elephant's tail and explains all the others were wrong. An elephant is like a rope.

Each man has his own perspective of the elephant. Each is different from the others, and all are correct. Their individual experience incorrectly causes them to feel the others are wrong, though. Only with sight of the full animal can we understand the holistic animal. Context and the level of our view biases our perspective.

When we're in a situation with others who disagree with our ideas or approach, remember the banana, the elephant, and the young and old women. Each of us is limited in our perspective, based on our experiences. With this reminder, we can pause, ask genuine questions about others' perspectives, and graciously discuss options to move forward, even when that path forward differs from our original preference.

Consider asking your team members these questions when in a contentious conversation.

How did you arrive at your perspective?

What else can you share to help me understand your approach?

What can we learn from each of our perspectives to help us achieve our goal?

CHAPTER 7:
SET GOALS ALIGNED TO PURPOSE

Situated almost 700 miles southeast of the US city of Miami, a tropical island sits within the Caribbean Sea. White-sand beaches line areas of the coast, giving access to crystal clear turquoise water. Step out of the water toward the land and you will be greeted with coconut trees and distant views of the mountains, which cover 70 percent of the island.

These mountains have formed from millions of years of volcanic activity and the Earth's shifting crusts, causing the land to rise above the water. One peak stands almost 9,000 feet above sea level. While areas of these mountains remain lush with conifers and mangroves, most of the trees have been removed to provide fuel for inhabitants.

The island is also one of the most densely populated with humans in the world, with more than 1,000 people per square mile. This is 11 times more people per square mile than in the United States and 57 percent more than nearby Jamaica[109]. Sadly, nearly nine in ten of the people on the island are estimated to live in poverty, with an average annual income of only $1,240. These residents are also subjected to severe political instability[110].

This island is Haiti.

The combined effects of being an isolated small island, environmental degradation, sitting above volcanic activity, and hosting high population density, widespread poverty, and political turmoil make Haiti uniquely vulnerable to natural disasters. When disaster hits this island nation, Haitians are heavily dependent on support from outsiders.

On January 12, 2010, a magnitude 7.0 earthquake in Haiti left more than 300,000 people dead and injured an additional 300,000[111]. Many of the country's buildings were destroyed, including hospitals, schools, and homes. The most significant damage occurred in Port-au-Prince, Haiti's capital. Dead bodies were strewn in the street. Those who remained either fled the city or tried their best to survive in its rubble. Some collected drinking water from broken pipes and distributed ice on the streets, since much of the infrastructure was destroyed[112].

Haitians desperately needed support, spurring the largest humanitarian intervention sent to any single nation at the time. More than 70 percent of the world's governments and 1,000 nonprofit organizations provided support. Access to Port-au-Prince was difficult, with few roads to allow entrance by large trucks and only one runway open at the airport. Many humanitarian assistance organizations struggled to gain access to those in need during the first weeks following the earthquake.

Medecins Sans Frontieres (MSF), known as Doctors Without Borders in the US, fortunately already had 800 field staff working in Port-au-Prince[113]. Existing MSF staff were able to administer medical treatment for the injured within hours and secured thousands of additional staff in the following weeks, many of them Haitian[114]. Since

60 percent of Haiti's healthcare facilities were destroyed in the earthquake, MSF staff had to establish new treatment centers, including an inflatable hospital on a football field.

Within less than a year following the earthquake, MSF teams conducted 16,570 surgeries and treated 358,000 patients overall. Some of the surgeries were lifesaving, including at least 140 amputations within a month of the disaster.

Adding to the difficulty of helping Haitians harmed by the earthquake, cholera broke out across Haiti nine months later, presumably the result of drinking contaminated water. At the time, this was the worst recorded cholera outbreak globally, with nearly one in ten Haitians getting cholera and 10,000 dying[115] [116]. MSF staff treated 60 percent of these cases, while continuing to serve those harmed by the earthquake.

MSF staff saved lives and improved conditions in Haiti before and after the 2010 earthquake, and they provide similar support around the world.

In 1971, a group of doctors and journalists in France founded MSF in response to war and famine in Nigeria. The 13 founding members worked alongside 300 volunteers to provide high quality healthcare regardless of gender, race, religion, creed, or political affiliation[117]. From the beginning, MSF also made a commitment to "bear witness" to their experience and speak up to increase awareness about problems they see.

This idea of bearing witness permeates the culture and is one of MSF's guiding principles, in which they share: "When the world turns its back on crises, we are duty-bound to raise our voices and speak out on behalf of our patients. Our decision to do so is always guided by our mission to do no harm, preserve respect and dignity, and protect life and health[118]." During his 1999 Nobel Peace Prize acceptance speech

President of the MSF International Council, Dr. James Orbinski reinforced MSF's commitment to speak up: "We are not sure that words can always save lives, but we know that silence can certainly kill[119]."

MSF recognizes the power of speaking up to support those they serve. Although they do not call it psychological safety, I think it is fair to say MSF has ingrained psychological safety into their work.

MSF has clear expectations for their workforce, combining high standards for patient care and an environment that encourages speaking up. Through this combination, the organization creates the space for collaboration and challenging, honest, and open dialogue that creates a team and work environment conducive to achieving difficult goals like saving lives. I suspect this is a significant reason MSF is able to hire medical professionals with high levels of altruism, flexibility, and intrinsic resilience[120].

We can all replicate and thrive from what MSF has modeled. The best teams I managed at Google, along with top performing companies that maintain psychologically safe environments have approaches that align with the MSF model. We are at our best when we are given aspirational goals to achieve and the ability to communicate openly throughout the journey to achieve those goals, even when things aren't going well.

Three things stand out in MSF's goal setting and how they work to achieve those goals, which align very well with my experience creating psychological safety within teams at Google. MSF focuses on why they do their work, not just how or what they do. They share clear expectations for staff, invite feedback, and listen to their ideas for improvement. And they trust the staff to co-create the approach to achieve their goal of providing medical support for those in need. Leadership doesn't always dictate the approach.

What larger goal do you work toward beyond your daily tasks?

Focus on the "Why"

MSF is in a unique position to identify a clear rationale for their work. The staff are in each country to provide medical support to those who otherwise would not receive it. Their purpose naturally aligns to intrinsic motivators of altruism and working through ambiguous challenges. These motivators result in improved human health for those they serve, and for many staff, a meaningful and positive life experience.

As we learned earlier about motivation, each of us can be inspired toward action in the short term by extrinsic motivators. Competitions and bonuses are great short-term motivators and can play an important role in business. But we are more likely to maintain long-term motivation when our work is aligned to intrinsic motivators. When intrinsically motivated, we will continue to pursue a difficult target, even in the absence of significant external rewards. This is what we see with MSF staff in Haiti, where many continue to help Haitians despite sometimes lower pay and unfavorable living conditions.

When we focus on why we do our work, our secondary focus then falls to what we're trying to achieve and how we do it. According to Simon Sinek, New York Times best-selling author and inspirational speaker, we appeal to our human biology when we start with why we are pursuing a target[121]. In doing so we immediately inspire the primary drivers of motivation.

We might feel challenged to start our target-setting conversations with why we're pursuing them. In my experience, we're much more likely to lead with what we need to achieve, and then immediately focus on achieving the goal.

I'll share a simplified Google example, understanding the difficulty of drawing too close a comparison between the business driven by Google Ads and the lifesaving work of MSF. My intent is to share how every business can benefit from leading with why we do the work, not to imply advertising is equivalent to saving lives.

When we have purpose in our work we are more likely to be intrinsically motivated and produce better outcomes.

Consider a Google Ads sales team that has received a $20 million target for next quarter. As a leader, I have a variety of ways I can share this target with the team and ask them to achieve it. We'll consider two approaches, the first leading with what we need to achieve, and the second leading with why we are being asked to achieve it.

In Google Ads sales, our "what" we need to achieve is simple: ad sales. Our "why" was often to support our customers' objectives. This might mean helping a large public corporation increase profitability in support of their stockholders, or helping a start-up increase sales volume to prove product viability to potential investors. In each scenario, the goal is unique to the customer and often independent of Google. When we helped them succeed, we were also more likely to benefit Google with ongoing advertising spending because we helped the client achieve their goals, and the sales team was therefore more likely to achieve their targets.

When we started with a focus on our customer, the individual, team, and Google success followed.

Option 1, our What: We need to sell $20 million in ads next quarter, and we'll work together to create a plan to hit this target. We're contributing to the broader Google revenue goal, and we should try to help our customers achieve their goals while we work toward ours.

Option 2, our Why: In the next three months, we have the opportunity to help our customers achieve their goals. We will work together to learn the customers' goals and identify the best ways to help them succeed with Google Ads. If we do this well, we'll increase the likelihood of achieving our $20 million sales target next quarter and support Google's overall revenue goals.

The phrasing might feel subtle, but the order plays an important role in how we think about achieving the goal, which directly relates to motivation. The phrase we lead with is most likely to dictate what happens next.

The "what" is tactical and uninspiring, encouraging the sales team to simply sell as many Google Ads as possible. Teams that focus here tend to get bored in their jobs due to repetition of the same sales pitch. These teams are also less successful over time because clients become frustrated with the tedious repetition of product overviews.

The "why" is creative and motivating. The sales team that focuses on their customer's needs must develop personal relationships, understand what matters to them and help to achieve their goals. Each conversation is nuanced and tailored to help others, not just the sales team. The client is more likely to achieve their goals and enjoy the personal connection, thus building mutual success over time.

What is your "why?"

 How do you currently phrase your goals for yourself and the team?

How can you begin to incorporate why you are pursuing your goals into more conversations?

Discuss Targets

MSF sets clear guiding principles that align to the organization's mission to provide medical attention to those in need. They then typically ask for feedback from the staff. Leadership realizes the staff in each location is more likely to observe the needs of those they serve. The staff is better equipped to recognize when things are going well, so they can share the success with others. They can also identify problems and support solutions in a way offsite leadership is unable. With staff input, MSF can then reflect on their successes and failures to continually work to maintain their efficacy, quality, and efficiency. The organization embraces all conversations, including those around failures, in order to improve.

In 2017, MSF staff supported more than 700,000 persecuted Rohingya people in a Bangladesh refugee camp[122]. They arrived at a crowded camp where hand water pumps were at risk for pulling contaminated drinking water from the same aquifer as the latrines[123]. So, MSF quickly began to research how they could source clean water for the refugees. Their onsite team assessed the best approach in close collaboration with MSF operational centers and other staff worldwide.

Leadership provides guidance and support, but then appears to forgo any ego in these situations. They put high trust in the feedback from the team on site as they establish their goals. This all goes back to the expectation that MSF staff bear witness, speak up, and share ideas to achieve the best outcomes.

This approach is applicable to nearly all work environments and is the crux of psychological safety. In my experience, the period of target setting is one of the most important times for leadership to proactively invite feedback, create the space for staff to share ideas, and to actively listen.

Target setting typically signals the start of something, so this can feel like a natural time to open a discussion about options. It can also inspire strong emotions, since target setting is difficult to get right. When setting targets, leadership is trying to predict the future and match the requests of their teams with the realities of the business. They hope to find the right balance of an aspirational, motivational goal, and the ability to potentially achieve it. But this doesn't always go as planned.

When a team receives a target that feels easily achievable, they might feel relaxed but also a little unmotivated to begin the work needed to achieve it. Why start working hard now, when we can relax at the start and not worry about it? When they receive a target that feels too difficult, they might feel overwhelmed and disheartened, assuming leadership doesn't understand or appreciate all the challenges they face. The team might feel fear that a failed target achievement will inhibit their next promotion or bonus and make them look unfavorable versus their peers. They might also feel unmotivated because they assume they'll be unable to hit the goal, even if they put in the effort.

In each of these scenarios, an open dialogue will allow each individual to express how they're feeling, the manager to proactively identify any challenges, and for the team to collaborate and identify the best path toward achieving their target.

If the team or manager doesn't create the psychological safety to discuss these challenges and move forward effectively as a team, the team members are unlikely to feel heard and will experience anxiety. As we learned earlier, if even one person on the team feels anxious, emotional contagion can spread the anxiety to others, which will further inhibit their ability to achieve the target.

For MSF, this difficulty could arise when staff are asked to overcome a serious challenge of getting fresh water to refugees, or life-saving supplies to Haiti. For Google, this could be about how to achieve an ads sales target that feels unachievable. In these moments, the start of the conversation often falls upon the manager to invite feedback.

Since the manager is typically responsible for overseeing the team's target achievement, she is similarly impacted and likely also has a shared initial emotional response with the team members. She can open the conversation with the team by disclosing her personal feelings and concerns. She can share if she also feels initially overwhelmed by leadership's expectations. This vulnerability, if genuine, invites connection with others and opens the dialogue for the team members to also share their thoughts.

Brené Brown, Research Professor of Social Work at the University of Houston, is a leader in research related to shame, vulnerability, and leadership. She has found that vulnerability can feel challenging, but is also "the birthplace of joy, of creativity, of belonging, of love[124]." When we are vulnerable, we embrace uncertainty, imperfection, and difficulties, and we allow others to see us for who we are, all of which help to invite psychological safety. This embrace of vulnerability and openness is the key to creating psychological safety during these challenging moments.

By acknowledging the challenge and discussing our vulnerabilities, we are better equipped to understand the source of the difficulty and then collaborate to find solutions. During my time at Google, I regularly acknowledged if I was struggling and shared how I was working through it in order to create a better outcome in the future. Like most things we experience at work, target achievement difficulties are usually temporary.

In these moments I tried to also empathize with the leadership that set the targets, as they're typically doing their best to balance overall company success with the support of the teams that drive that success. They're human and will not always get it right but in my experience, most care about their people and business results. Once we begin to think of others and the broader company context, we can start to consider new perspectives to our situation, which inspires creativity and innovation[125]. Through this expanded view of our situation and target setting, we're better equipped to find new approaches to achieve our targets.

Now that the team has seen the manager's vulnerability and better understands the context for the creation of their targets, they are more likely to feel comfortable sharing their perspectives and ideas to move forward. This is a great time to guide the team through the three stages of building psychological safety.

Invite: After modeling how to express concern with vulnerability, the manager can ask team members to share their thoughts. She might not ask all of these questions, but here are a few examples of open-ended questions to invite conversation. How do you feel about the upcoming targets? What are your concerns? What opportunity do you see to support your customers? How can this customer support help us achieve our target? How would you approach the next three months to ensure team well-being and happiness? What steps would you take in the first month of the quarter to help us exceed our target in three months?

Each team member might have different preferences for if and how they share their perspective. This can be a delicate balance of creating the space to have the discussion, while not forcing anyone to do something that causes undue discomfort. Some team members might thrive in a group discussion, openly sharing their ideas and concerns with the full team. Others might prefer a more private one-to-one discussion or email, where they can take the time to write the words that best reflect what they are feeling.

The manager can reinforce the team's psychological safety by offering communication options that align to each team member's preference. She can ask them how they feel most comfortable sharing.

All of this has dual intentions—to ensure everyone has the opportunity to be heard, and to improve the likelihood of success achieving the target. Both are only possible if the manager truly listens to the team members.

Share: Once she has prompted the discussion and asked each team member how they feel most comfortable sharing feedback, the manager now allows the team to share with her. Her goal is to listen to their ideas and genuinely consider what they share, without judgment. This is a time for the team to talk and the manager to listen.

For some this might be a time to vent their fears, disappointments, and anger, which can temporarily help to reduce our stress. It can also create connections and sharing among team members, but it's insufficient to help us move forward productively[126]. So, venting should be quickly followed with a more productive path forward that acknowledges challenges but shifts the team's energy toward model examples of success.

Listen: The simple act of listening without judgment can help build and reinforce psychological safety since it allows everyone to be heard and understood. Through these conversations, the manager will likely uncover new perspectives, identify resource gaps the team needs filled to succeed, and collect new ideas to achieve the targets. She also might feel personally challenged at times, if the team feels uncomfortable with a component of her leadership.

All of this feedback is important, as it allows everyone to openly discuss the opportunities and challenges facing the team. Just like in Pixar's Braintrust, the manager hears, acknowledges, and respects each perspective. The manager will then work with the team to finalize the path forward, with the final decision coming from her in most cases.

At this point, the team has set a goal aligned to a purpose, with a focus on why they are asked to achieve it. They also have had the opportunity to share how they feel about the target and their ideas to achieve it. I would not expect any of these discussions to result in an adjusted target, but like MSF, a successful manager will anchor the target in something meaningful and will create the space to discuss the best approach to achieve it. The team is now equipped to consider the journey forward.

What concerns do you have about collecting feedback about target-setting? What is one step you can take to alleviate your concerns?

How will you share feedback during the next target-setting process? How will you collect feedback from others?

CHAPTER 8:
SUPPORT THE PATH FORWARD

The path toward target achievement is often simultaneously personal and shared across the team. Each individual has her unique skills, experiences, life-stages, desires to learn, and ability to contribute. The combination of these experiences, abilities, and motivations from each person come together to create the team. In a psychologically safe team, a manager will account for individual differences while maintaining the space for open communication, ultimately bringing the team together to work toward the shared goal.

Even the most experienced and respected leader is more likely to drive company success if she sets targets aligned to purpose and then allows the input and co-creation of target achievement from her team.

Just as MSF had to prioritize effort to achieve the greatest impact in both Haiti and Bangladesh, most of us need to make difficult decisions about where to spend our time. A similar type of prioritization needs to happen in most work environments. We have to make many decisions during our efforts to hit targets, which can be loosely generalized into two types. The first are larger decisions that require group alignment, often relating to higher level strategy. The second are often more individual and recurring, where each of us must decide how to dedicate our working time within each day.

We will consider our Google Ads sales team again. Each team member already understands the purpose behind their sales target–to help their customers achieve their goals. If they effectively match Google's ad products to the goals of their customers, they are more likely to achieve their $20 million sales goal.

This alignment to customer success is a great starting point, but it's insufficient to guide team members especially newer to the job toward what to do next. Many will need more specific guidance. Imagine a team member who is responsible for supporting twenty Google advertisers. He might struggle to know where to dedicate his effort for the biggest customer impact. The same is true for a team member who is responsible for only one really large customer that has complex relationships within the company and across their advertising agencies.

The next step is to provide a path forward for the team and empower each individual to make choices aligned to the purpose-filled target. We create psychological safety through the resulting discussions, with everyone sharing ideas for the best path forward.

Throughout these decisions, the team will consider tradeoffs. Each of us has a finite amount of time to work productively each day. Each of us is also more productive and makes fewer mistakes when we focus on one task at a time, so we will assume nobody will attempt the myth of productive multitasking[127]. For every task we pursue, we are unable to pursue another. This makes our prioritization even more important, since some tasks are more likely to provide a greater impact than others.

Align on Group Decision-making

Some decisions are likely to include multiple team members or management. For our example, a Google Ads team could support twenty customers, each possibly having different goals and varying ability for the Google team to support those goals. Each team member might have different perspectives on where to focus their effort, with some wanting to work toward short-term success—quick wins for the customer and sales team. Others might want to develop relationships that will help the customer and team achieve future goals. To be successful, the team needs to ensure their efforts are best aligned to achieve the customers' and the team's goals, now and in the future. The manager can play a key role here, helping to establish the approach to decision-making that brings everyone along.

Mike Figliuolo is an honor graduate from West Point and founder of a nationally recognized organization for public speaking and training[128]. He leads training for many companies, where he introduces and helps activate his company's approach for decision-making. He's helped many large and multinational corporate teams align toward and achieve common goals by removing ambiguity around the decision-making process. In each moment where a decision is required, my teams and I would select one of four options based on Figliuolo's decision-making styles: autocratic, participatory, democratic, or consensus based.

Of the four styles, I have a strong bias toward participatory decision-making whenever possible, since it's explicitly designed to build psychological safety through open dialogue, discussion, and feedback. But each has its own merits.

Autocratic: A single person or small group makes the decision and others follow. This works well when there is a clear and unambiguous goal that everyone needs to work to achieve, like the growth goals for a whole company that are communicated to external stakeholders. The autocratic principle can also work well in situations where a decision must be made quickly, even with incomplete information. But I have seen this form of decision-making inhibit psychological safety because it does not invite open discussion or feedback.

Participatory: Members of a team contribute ideas and preferences. A single person or small group makes the final decision, influenced by the team members' contributions. This principle works well for things like planning to achieve targets where the team has already aligned around goals and priorities, but then needs to finalize ownership and timelines. While no decision-making process is perfect and all have tradeoffs, I find participatory decision-making to inspire the highest feelings of psychological safety and Google agrees. Google's re:Work publication about psychological safety encourages decision makers to solicit and acknowledge input from teammates and to explain the rationale for the decision made[129]. By definition, participatory decision-making asks everyone to share their perspective, independent of their role or level on the team. While the final decision will be made by a leader or small group, everyone's voice is heard with participatory decision-making, influencing that leader's decision-making process.

Democratic: Team members vote and the majority wins. This approach can be perceived as fair because it allows the majority to dictate the action, but this can also inhibit psychological safety for those who are in the minority. Since their voice and influence won't impact or change the outcome, those in the minority are not incentivized to share their perspective. In teams composed mostly of White males, as is common in the tech world, democratic decision-making has a risk of inhibiting the voice of women and people of color.

Consensus-based: All team members agree on the decision. This can sometimes work well for smaller groups, but rarely is feasible for larger teams. In my experience on diverse teams with unique perspectives, this is rarely an option for effective decision-making. I have also seen it inhibit psychological safety, particularly when the manager has expressed a strong desire for the team to arrive at consensus. Consensus can inhibit the expression of contrary ideas due to a desire to join the groupthink of the team. This can allow leadership to move forward with the delusion of consensus, with dissenters unintentionally silenced.

Once we have established how we'll make decisions, we can try to identify bright spots.

Chip Heath is Professor Emeritus, Organizational Behavior at Stanford University[130]. Dan Heath is a Senior Fellow at Duke University[131] and is Chip's brother. The Heath brothers have partnered to write three *New York Times* bestsellers, including *Switch*, which encourages us to replicate successes over fixing problems[132]. Instead of focusing on how to avoid failure, the successful team will acknowledge the challenges they face but then focus their energy on finding examples of and emulating success. When we focus on success, we are more likely to establish a positive road map for action to achieve a goal, instead of wasting that same energy and time avoiding failure. These successes are called "bright spots."

If a team aligns on participatory decision-making with the pursuit of bright spots, every team member knows their ideas will influence decisions, with the hope of creating positive energy to align everyone around shared priorities. Few group operational decisions reach a nirvana of everyone feeling perfectly aligned, but this process creates the space for that conversation. Through the open discussion, each team member can comfortably share their concerns about the decision, allowing the manager and other team members to partner to address the concern as they all move forward together.

The team now knows the path forward, and they will need to begin their individual contributions. This requires another layer of decision-making—what to do with the limited time of each workday.

How does your team currently make decisions?

How can you support a more inclusive decision-making process in the future?

Empower Team Members to Take Action

Not all effort is made equal. Some efforts will help customers and the team achieve their goals. Others will result in neither.

Imagine that a Google Ads team member starts her day at 8:00 a.m. and is immediately greeted with forty new emails. These emails include requests from another Google team for her to help with a project going to a Vice President, a sales-skills training that must be completed in the next 48 hours, several new product updates and case studies to review, industry articles about her customers, and questions from her customers about their advertising campaigns. She also needs to build a presentation for an upcoming customer meeting, meet with five customers for their weekly call, attend an internal team planning meeting, and sit through a planning session for a team fun-event.

She stares at the screen for a moment and already feels overwhelmed, unsure how to dedicate her time for the next eight working hours. Instead of starting her work, she steps away from the computer, takes a deep breath, and attempts to garner the energy for the work ahead with a big cup of coffee.

Her experience might sound familiar, with a daunting list of work requirements impacting many of us. Adding to the difficulty of prioritizing effort and completing our many work tasks, we're distracted at least every half-hour by texts, email, internet browsing, and unplanned conversations with co-workers[133]. Some studies have found we are distracted even more regularly, checking our phones every 12 minutes[134]. Many tasks might simultaneously feel urgent. The high quantity of required work tasks combined with all the distractions can lead to us feeling overwhelmed and stressed by work.

Dwight Eisenhower, the 34th president of the United States, shared an appropriate comment that can help in these moments: "What is important is seldom urgent and what is urgent is seldom important.[135]" This attribution led to a helpful decision-making 2 by 2 diagram called the Eisenhower Method, made popular by Stephen Covey, A. Roger Merrill, and Rebecca Merrill in their best-selling book *First Things First*[136]. The diagram was further adapted to the 4 Ds of time management (Do, Delay, Delegate, Drop). Covey describes our desire to complete urgent tasks as like using an addictive drug. When we complete an urgent task we feel useful, successful, and validated, causing us to crave that feeling again, often at the expense of things we consider more important. How many times has a work deadline pulled you away from time with family, which you value more than the work project? When was the last time the ping of a text or social media alert caused you to pause an in-person conversation to look at your phone? Urgency and importance play key roles in how we function each day and what we accomplish, but many of us fail to recognize what is actually driving our behavior.

This time management framework can help us recognize what we are experiencing and can create an opportunity to discuss our approach with our team and manager. It can help us identify what tasks to complete now versus later, empowering team members–whether those devoted to MSF emergency response or Google Ads team members dedicating their time to the most impactful sales efforts–to choose their paths of action. We can categorize our effort into four quadrants.

Do: tasks that provide the highest impact and require immediate attention

Delay: tasks that are impactful but can be delayed temporarily with relatively less harm

Delegate: tasks that feel pressing but are not essential for success

Drop: tasks that are neither impactful nor time sensitive, so time devoted to them is wasted

The 2 by 2 approach would benefit the Google Ads team member who is feeling overwhelmed by the number of tasks she hopes to complete. The most important tasks will be those that support her customer's goals while contributing to her target achievement. So, she'll dedicate her effort toward the customer-facing tasks, delay her review of the product updates and skills training, try to find others to contribute to the internal meeting and VP project, and she'll remove herself from the event planning. Since she knows achieving her customer's goals is the most important part of her effort to achieve targets, she can more easily segment her work and reduce the burden she feels.

	Urgent	Not Urgent
Important	**DO** Respond to customer questions & meet with five customers Build presentation for upcoming customer meeting Review industry articles about customers, to see if any goals have changed or are at risk	**DELAY** Review new product updates and case-studies Complete required sales skills training
Not Important	**DELEGATE** Attend internal meeting Support other Google team with their VP project	**DROP** Fun event planning

Figure 6: Example of decision-making for a Google Ads team member, prioritizing the most urgent and important tasks before others.

When we combine a purpose-based target, clear decision-making, and the ability to identify the most urgent and important tasks aligned to the purpose, we help each team member take individual aligned steps toward target achievement. This reinforces psychological safety by encouraging ongoing dialogue about how to best achieve goals while supporting personal well-being.

What are the most important and urgent tasks on your to-do list?

What can you Delay? Delegate? Drop?

Make the Plan Accessible

Now that everyone is aligned on the path forward and knows they can continue to share ideas to achieve the target, it is time to document and communicate the plan. This often shows up as a project plan. If you ask my previous teams how they feel about this stage, I expect you'd receive mixed reviews. Some greatly appreciated the transparency and clear understanding of expectations, while others felt documenting a plan might stifle their creativity and flexibility.

I empathize with these concerns and sometimes have similar feelings, either way. Project plans can feel restrictive and controlling if they are inflexible. But when done well, a project plan can actually enhance creativity[137]! Over the last 15 years, I have seen the benefits of a good project plan consistently outweigh the challenges.

A good project plan will include clear expectation setting and recurring invitations to reassess. The expectation setting often shows up as tasks needed to achieve the target, timelines, success metrics at each stage of the plan, and identification of who is responsible for completing the task. In a team environment, the person responsible for completing the task isn't necessarily expected to work alone. They should often include others' perspectives and expertise to complete the task, and even ask for others to complete portions of the task when appropriate. But they are responsible for the task completion and for communicating any challenges to their manager.

Atul Gawande is a best-selling author, renowned surgeon, Harvard Medical School professor, and public health leader[138]. In *The Checklist Manifesto*, one of Gawande's best-selling books, he shares the importance of checklists to help teams avoid failures and align effort toward common goals[139]. A Google search shows us project plans can take many forms, with most showing up as a checklist.

We live in a world that requires many of us to keep track of a volume and complexity of information that we're unable to consistently remember without an aid. Add distractions of texts, social media, email, and unplanned conversations and we're even more likely to veer off task and make mistakes in our work. This complexity and the consistent distractions in our lives can even impact our IQ. One study showed distractions from our email caused twice the IQ reduction of smoking marijuana[140]. While this comparison might be a bit sensationalized, it's a great reminder about the negative influence of distractions on our ability to focus.

Companies often try to solve the problem of information complexity and distractions with training and knowledge sharing. This tactic can unfortunately make the problem even worse, adding more information to our already complex world.

A checklist can remove some of this mental burden through simple documentation of our goals and process, thus increasing focus on the highest priority efforts. When captured in an openly accessible and shared document, the checklist also provides an easy way for everyone to track progress. At Google, we would often build these plans in a Google Sheet or Doc and share with each team member. Everyone on the team could monitor progress independently, and we could then bring that informed perspective into our weekly team meetings, where we discussed our progress and any obstacles to overcome. The project plan supported our ongoing conversations, further reinforcing the psychological safety within the group to share ideas for improvement.

When one team member is excelling and ahead of the plan, they can celebrate their progress and use any additional time to share their best-practices with others on the team or within the company. When a team member encounters a challenge, the team and manager can work together to identify the appropriate support to help them continue moving forward.

In my experience, the most successful project plans contain the following components:

Alignment: Each of the checklist steps contribute directly to the success of the team's purpose-based target. Each step has been identified as something on which the team members need to take an action categorized as either Do, Delay, or Delegate. Nothing identified as Drop should make it into the checklist.

Simplification: Each step is a single action, with each subsequent action building on the one before it. Consider a team member who needs to build new relationships with a customer before she can propose a meeting. Her first step will be to contact the people necessary to enable the meeting. The next step will be to schedule the meeting. Each team member will have concurrent actions to move the team toward their goals. Regular check-ins can ensure alignment and identify required areas to adjust the strategy.

Clarity: Each step has a single owner and deadline. The deadlines account for other work that needs to be completed, providing working time plus a buffer in case things do not go as planned. I have a bias toward a single owner for most action items we encounter at work, with that person being responsible for including others as needed, in support of achieving the goal. I've seen this single ownership model support improved psychological safety and motivation for the team. The team member has the autonomy to pursue the work and openly discuss progress as needed to achieve it along the way. Particularly in project management roles I've seen a strong opposing opinion though, with many preferring a RACI model. RACI allocates effort across a group of individuals who are identified as (R)esponsible, (A)ccountable, (C)onsulted, or (I)nformed. In my experience, this model causes a diffusion of responsibility where roles become unclear and the desired action takes longer to achieve, often with confused roles along the way. But each team will need to determine what works best for them.

Forecasting: The checklist helps to set expectations for the team and their leadership about their progress, what they've completed, and what they'll pursue. It can help to determine if the team is on track to achieve their targets. If they aren't on track, the team can then assess what they can change in their project plan to improve the potential result. They can also use the checklist to communicate their expected results and strategy to leadership and others who might have interest in the outcomes.

I've shared a simple example project plan checklist below for a team member named Carlos. Carlos is responsible for developing new customer relationships to help the customer build market awareness about their new product launch. A full team project plan would include each team member's responsibilities, allowing the team to identify and discuss areas of potential overlap and partnership.

- (Due: April 2; Owner: Carlos) Identify who at the customer is responsible for launching the new product.
- (Due: April 16; Owner: Carlos) Schedule meetings with at least three senior leaders aligned to the product launch.
- (Due: April 30; Owner: Carlos) Meet with at least three senior leaders aligned to the product launch to understand the customer's product launch timing, their sales goals for the new product launch, and current plans to achieve those goals.
- (Due: May 14; Owner: Carlos) Develop an advertising strategy to support the customer's product launch goals, with a focus on building awareness to drive sales.
- (Due: May 21; Owner: Carlos) Schedule a customer meeting,

including all decision-making stakeholders to share the proposed advertising strategy, collect customer feedback, and align on next steps.

- (Due: June 4; Owner: Carlos) Activate the agreed upon advertising strategy and track new product sales. Adjust as needed.

With the processes shared above and a genuine invitation from the manager to share feedback along the way, these goals and checklists help to create a shared language across the team. When everyone is aware of the goals and steps to achieve them, they can refer to something tangible and can understand the progression toward the goals. They can also use that language as a starting point to consider alternative options. In some cases a team member might feel very strongly that a proposed plan is wrong. When they have a written checklist, they can more easily articulate what is missing or wrong with the existing plan and begin to explore alternative solutions. This anchoring provides a starting point for a conversation, and with the invitation from the manager, acts as a prompt for sharing questions, concerns, and mistakes.

How could a checklist align your team toward their goals? How could the checklist support ongoing discussion?

What resonates from this project plan approach? What, if anything, would you change?

Acknowledge the Group's Journey

The individuals within the team share a path as they learn what is expected of them, discuss anticipated challenges, agree to how they will make decisions, prioritize their efforts, and begin to implement their plan. Similar to how the individual learning journey brings us from Anticipating to Automatic, many teams go through a journey from Connect to Champion (Figure 7). This pathway is particularly applicable to a team composed of at least some new team members but can also apply when the team reacts to a change. Once off the pathway, they might begin on it again if the expectations of them significantly change, the team gets a new leader, or after the company experiences change, like a reorganization or merger.

If we understand the group journey, we are better equipped to discuss and improve our experience.

CONNECT	CHALLENGE	COLLABORATE	CHAMPION
Meet teammates. Learn goals.	Question approach. Assert opinions.	Work together. Feel trust.	Support others. Feel safe.

Beginning of team relationships   High performing team

Figure 7: Many successful teams follow a developmental pathway that begins with establishing relationships and progresses through identifying differences on the way to high performance.

No framework is universally applicable, including this one. But I invite you to find the components that resonate.

Connect: When we first join a team, we often have no expectations of each other or feel pressure to achieve a shared goal. We can show up with an open mind, without judgment, or feelings of competition. We approach others with genuine curiosity and excitement.

Challenge: In my experience, this is the most important part of the team journey. It establishes the basis for future team success.

After we get to know each other and understand the work processes, we begin to bring forward stronger perspectives about how things should be done. We also start to enact our preferred ways of working. Through these stronger opinions and preferred working styles, we start to uncover differences with our teammates.

This is where psychological safety plays a key role in team development.

Many theories recognize the role of conflict in group development.[141] Business consultancies and academics often describe this phase with language that could be considered negative. They characterize it as the team phase filled with friction, clashes, challenges, and tension. One consultancy calls out that team members might even challenge leadership, resulting in hierarchical confrontations and simmering tensions. At its worst, this is also a stage of less active participation within the team, due to the negative feelings arising from conflict.

But I have a different perspective. The Challenge phase is the time to proactively identify differences in working styles, personalities, and goals. Instead of feeling concern and negativity, we can feel excitement and joy as we identify the diverse perspectives from across the team, and how each of those perspectives adds unique value to help us achieve our goals. If you haven't already, now is the time to openly discuss and align on those purpose-filled targets, decision-making, and the path forward.

While the discussions will inevitably include disagreements and temporary conflict, we can enjoy the process of uncovering and finding mutually beneficial outcomes through open communication. We can practice, build, and demonstrate the opportunity for each team member to share their ideas openly and without repercussions. If we approach the Challenge phase in this positive way, we can maintain high productivity and team happiness as we identify how each team member can best contribute to the team's and their personal goals.

A highly productive team will maintain and celebrate components of the Challenge phase throughout all phases of their team development. They will maintain the conditions to continually consider new ideas and approaches, even when those ideas introduce potential conflict. When we have high psychological safety, we embrace that conflict when it is based on best intentions aligned to supporting the individual and team's ongoing improvement.

Collaborate: As the team aligns on their path forward, they can begin to comfortably work toward their goals. In the Collaborate phase, the team feels more confident and assured. They trust other team members and continue to develop their feelings of psychological safety. This comfort and increased collaboration can also create the conditions for group think, if everyone agrees with each other. If this happens, the team can become complacent over time, missing important opportunities for growth and improvement. Each of us can watch for this and proactively introduce discussions to help move beyond the group think.

Champion: The team reaches this stage over time, as they continue their journey toward shared goals. Largely a result of the psychological safety demonstrated during a productive Challenge phase and continuing through the Collaborate phase, they now have culminated in a feeling of high personal motivation paired with a trust for the other team members. They work toward their individual and team success, recognizing they achieve even greater excellence by elevating those around them, not only themselves. The team continues to feel psychologically safe as they pursue their goals, often feeling like they are in a flow.

At the end of a temporary assignment, when a team member moves to a new role, or when the manager or company changes, the team can feel disrupted. In many cases, these changes cause each team member to experience the team differently than before, which can shift them to the Connect phase again.

I am not aware of many teams that remain static, particularly in today's work environment. So, each of us will likely experience this cycle many times in our careers, regularly shifting between phases within our teams. Rarely is the path a linear one.

In changing industries and workforces we regularly have to adjust to new teammates, often with different perspectives, preferences, and goals. We typically cannot control if a teammate takes a new job, or our company merges our department with another. But we can control how we approach and respond to these situations. We can encourage the development of psychological safety within each team and help team members find joy and success in the Challenge phase. Each of us can create a better team environment by inviting and embracing the diverse ideas around us, and we can do this better by recognizing where we are in the journey.

 In what part of the journey is your team?

How comfortable are you in the Challenge phase of the team journey? What steps can you take to shift any negative feelings toward positive feelings aligned to individual and team growth?

CHAPTER 9:
PARTNER FOR SUCCESS

On March 29, 1987, the Tennessee Volunteers (Vols) women's basketball team stepped onto the court for the national championship game for the second time. They faced Louisiana Tech, who had beaten them the last nine times and easily outscored the Vols just months before. The Vols were a great team. By the time they faced Louisiana Tech in the finals, they had amassed eleven consecutive seasons with at least twenty wins, but the national championship continued to elude them.

That day in March would be different.

The Vols led early and did not back down. Up by 11 points at halftime, they accelerated their lead to 19 points with four minutes remaining in the game. The deficit was insurmountable for Louisiana Tech, and the Vols won their first national championship by 23 points!

Pat Summitt led this championship team, and she didn't stop there. Summitt coached the Vols for 38 years and ended her career with 1,098 wins, the most of any college basketball head coach at the time of her retirement. She led her teams to 31 consecutive NCAA tournaments where they won eight championships, were runners-up five times, and secured 22 Final Fours. Summitt was awarded National Coach of the Year seven times and the SEC conference Coach of the Year eight times[142]. She is one of the best coaches of all time.

Summitt was known for being very tough. She expected a lot from the women on her teams. After one of the Vols' losses at Vanderbilt, the team boarded the bus and rode the nearly 200 miles back to Knoxville. Instead of resting when they returned, the team watched game film until at least two o'clock in the morning. Summitt then had the team get dressed for basketball again and had them complete running drills across the court. Those who played the worst against Vanderbilt had to run the most[143]. This happened the same year as the Vols won their first national championship.

Without context, her behavior might sound abusive. Having played sports for much of my life, I have met many punitive coaches who made us suffer without any apparent rationale. They punished us with seemingly no care or underlying lessons.

But the stories about Summitt make her seem different. She balanced her toughness with care. One of her best-known quotes summarizes this well. "People don't care how much you know until they know how much you care[144]." I cannot speculate how she expressed her care during those early morning hours after the Vanderbilt game, but based on what we know about Summitt's approach to coaching, we can reasonably assume she balanced that tough moment with many moments of care.

She demonstrated this care so well that, after she passed away in 2016, previous athletes recalled how she touched their lives. Summitt was celebrated as a coach, friend, mentor, and motivator, helping to build physical and mental strength[145]. Three-time WNBA champion

Candace Parker even described her as a "second mom.[146]" Her positive impact extended beyond the court.

Summitt modeled much of what we would expect from a leader who creates psychological safety. She set very clear goals for her teams, firmly stated her expectations, and continually communicated to help everyone improve over time. She even captured a code of conduct called the Definite Dozen, which outlined her philosophy[147]. While each component of the Definite Dozen aligned well with the creation of psychological safety, a few are uniquely relevant.

She expected each team member to take responsibility for their successes and failures, big and small. When we make ourselves accountable for mistakes, we can continually improve.

She expected everyone to learn to be a strong communicator. Communication includes speaking, listening, and body language, even when we are silent. Communication eliminates mistakes.

She acknowledged that change is constant. Through change, we can continually improve.

She also recognized the importance of learning from success and failure. We can't always control what happens, but we can control our response. We can often learn more from losing than we do from winning.

Pat Summitt became one of the best coaches of all time, at least in part by recognizing the importance of us taking responsibility for our failures, communicating openly to support ongoing improvement, embracing change, and learning from our experiences. The best leaders emulate what Pat Summitt brought to her teams. Just as we expect from an organization with high psychological safety, Summitt was honest and open with her feedback, even when she knew it was difficult to hear. We can replicate this in our teams at work if we learn to recognize when to communicate through feedback, coaching, and modeled behavior. Each of these can help to guide the team to achieve the shared purpose-filled goal we discussed above.

While managers and leadership play a disproportionate role in this, everyone within a team can play a role. In a psychologically safe team everyone wants to improve, including the manager. While a manager is on average more likely to have the experience and knowledge to enable her to share feedback, coach, and model behavior with the team, she'll also continue to improve if she genuinely embraces feedback from her team members.

In a long career, we'll likely experience moments where everything seems to go as planned. We achieve targets with relative ease and we receive that high performance rating aligned to the big bonus or promotion. But we'll also experience the opposite, where the work feels like a constant struggle, we fail to hit targets, and our performance review focuses mostly on ways we can improve. While it would be reasonable to feel more joy when things are going well, it's possible to feel happy and rewarded in both of these scenarios. The manager plays a key role, though. If she regularly communicates with her team, with the members' best intentions at the core of her approach, they'll recognize the positive long-term impact of feedback, even when it is critical.

A great leader will celebrate moments of success and critically review what led to the success, acknowledging what was driven by external factors and what was only made possible because of the team's effort. She can then educate others within the company about what worked for their team, helping everyone to achieve similar positive outcomes. That same leader will replicate this analysis in moments of failure, understanding what the team could have done better and what was out of their control. She'll do all of this with an understanding and sensitivity that, as humans, we are more heavily impacted by negative feedback. If she hopes to maintain a high-performing team she'll recognize that her team members will need a balance of more positive feedback than criticism[148].

Feedback and coaching are often conflated and are nearly always intertwined, since the intent behind both approaches overlaps. When done well, both support an individual's growth and performance through open dialogue. Feedback is more likely to be effective when comparing actual versus desired performance. Coaching can be effective at helping learners excel in the moment and achieve their potential over time.

Dr. Adelle Atkinson is a medical professor in Toronto who focuses her medical practice on pediatrics. In their review of feedback and coaching, Dr. Atkinson and her colleagues define feedback as a comparison between actual performance and a standard toward which the learner aspires. Coaching is more of a philosophy to help learners improve personal and professional performance over time through ongoing learning[149]. Feedback can be more situational, with personal coaching applied to both the short and long term, helping a learner to continually reflect and improve.

Since there are a variety of interpretations of feedback and coaching, I don't believe there is a single correct approach, but I have found the considerations below help me determine how to best support team members (Figure 8).

	Feedback	Coaching
Timing	In the moment	Ongoing
Communication	Direct statements about performance and ideas for improvement	Open ended questions to inspire reflection about ways to improve
Topics	More tactical, with potential for immediate behavior change	More aspirational, with a desire for ongoing improvement
Achieved (when done well)	Results in clear next steps Supports the learner's development Empowers psychological safety through open dialogue	

Figure 8: Feedback and coaching differ in their approach but can result in similar positive outcomes.

After you have navigated discussions aligned to setting targets and shared approaches to achieve those targets, I view ongoing communication to be the next most important connection between psychological safety and business outcomes.

Guide Improvement—Feedback

Feedback is when we share a reaction to or assessment of performance in a specific situation, often from a manager to a team member. It can celebrate what went well and support future improvement. Georgia Hardavella, a physician at the King's College Hospital in London, researched feedback with several global colleagues[150]. Their research reinforced and expanded on some aspects of a popular feedback framework attributed to Dr. David Pendleton and his colleagues[151]. A few of their findings aligned particularly well with what I observed as successful feedback at Google, when it's given:

- one-to-one
- promptly after the event
- with space for the recipient to reflect on the event and consider how they will improve in the future

This feedback process assumes a one-to-one interaction, with a facilitator and a learner. The facilitator—often a manager in a work situation—can be anyone who's in a position to effectively provide the feedback and is respected by the recipient. The learner—often a team member receiving the feedback from their manager—can be any of us who receive feedback from someone we respect.

An effective feedback approach commonly includes three components: an invitation to the discussion, a recognition of things that went well, and acknowledgement of those that can be improved. The manager and team member contribute to the feedback discussion, with both providing their own perspective. The manager tries to deliver the feedback when the team member is prepared for the discussion, ensuring they're in a mindset that allows them to receive the feedback well and are more likely to act on the critique to make future improvements. She can integrate a discussion about the context, actions, and desired results as they go through the process (Figure 9).

Confirm Timing: The manager confirms the team member is ready for feedback: "When is the best time this week for me to share some feedback?" When possible, the manager will try to accommodate the team member so they can receive the feedback at a time that is right for them. The manager then shares the situation they'll discuss and asks the team member to reflect on the situation and be ready to share their perspective.

Celebrate Success: This is the moment to identify and share what went well. If they are comfortable and able, the team member should share first. This ensures they arrive at their success story without being influenced by the manager's perspective. When a team member is newer to this process or significantly struggling to identify a success to share, the manager can share first. This can help to model the behavior and encourage the team member to feel comfortable, so they can then share first in a future feedback session.

The manager asks: "What is one thing that went well?" The team member shares one thing that went well. The manager then tells the team member one thing they think went well, including a reminder about the context, actions taken, and the positive results they achieved.

Invite Improvement: Now is the time to consider what the team member can do better in the future. Similar to sharing what went well, the team member should share their thoughts first when appropriate and they are able.

The manager asks: "What is one thing you would do differently?" The team member reflects and shares something they would like to improve next time. The manager then tells the team member one thing they can improve on in the future, including a reminder about the context, alternative actions they could demonstrate for more success, and the positive results those alternative actions could have.

The intent is not to rigidly apply this feedback approach to every situation, but to recognize the key components so we can acknowledge and replicate successes while identifying and finding future solutions to challenges. In a moment of excellence, it's reasonable for a manager to only highlight what went well and forgo the criticism. After an egregious and deliberate action that harmed others, she might be better off focusing only on how to improve.

Confirm Timing	Celebrate Success		Invite Improvement	
Manager: "When is the best time this week for me to share some feedback? I'd like to discuss your recent client presentation." **Team Member:** "Tomorrow morning at 10:00 works well for me."	**Manager:** Ask "What is one thing that went well?" **Team Member:** Share what they felt went well. "I spoke slowly to ensure everyone could follow what I presented."	**Manager:** Share what they felt went well. "You adjusted to the audience needs, pausing to answer questions during a complex portion of the presentation. This helped everyone feel aligned and ready to move forward."	**Manager:** Ask "What is one thing you would do differently?" **Team Member:** Share what they would change. "I would simplify the presentation to make it easier to understand and reduce the need for questions."	**Manager:** Share what they would do differently. "You could send an overview of the presentation 48 hours before you present. This would give the audience the opportunity to review the content and arrive more prepared."

Figure 9: In this example feedback flow, the manager and team member discuss successes and areas to improve, aligned to the context, actions taken, and expected results of the situation.

This approach to feedback requires that the manager understand the context and details of the situation in order to provide valuable input on the desired actions and expected results. To be effective, feedback should be based on firsthand observations.

When leading teams at Google, I gained this context by co-leading meetings with team members, shadowing calls, and listening to client-call recordings. The team member leaves a successful feedback session with clear ideas to consider for future performance, including positive reinforcement for where they performed well and clear guidance for where they can continue to improve. The manager also gains from the interaction since they leave the feedback session with a better understanding of the team member's perspective about their performance and abilities. All of this promotes psychological safety by encouraging open discussions about the things that are going well and those that can be improved upon.

Feedback is great at helping to guide ongoing improvement and can be particularly helpful supporting team members newer to a role or experience, as it can guide them toward successful behaviors. While effective feedback includes some reflection from the team member, it relies heavily on the manager to provide ideas for improvement. We'll review coaching next, which shifts the impetus for improvement ideas to the team member, inspired by open-ended questions from the manager.

How many times did you provide feedback in the last week? How many times did you invite reflection when you gave feedback?

What opportunities will you pursue in the next week to provide feedback?

Inspire Reflection—Coaching

Feedback is great for moments where a manager can share tactical ways to improve or celebrate successes to support ongoing great performance, but it can feel more transactional than coaching. Coaching compliments feedback by encouraging more personal reflection, as the team member works toward their longer-term growth and improvement. Instead of sharing direct ideas for improvement, as the manager would in feedback, coaching relies more on open-ended questions to help the team member identify their own proposed solutions and next steps.

Many of us are taught early in our careers to focus on tasks. A salesperson might be asked to focus on achieving a revenue target, an engineer to focus on writing code, an accountant to balance the books, and a pediatrician to maintain the health of her young patients. Feedback often focuses on the specific actions taken to achieve the goals unique to our roles. A good coach helps expand our focus beyond these tactics into understanding the broader impact of our work, guiding us to consider alternative approaches. Through coaching, the salesperson can understand how her contributions impact the whole organization, how the engineer's code will improve the larger existing network, the accountant will support ongoing company operations, and how the pediatrician is empowering a new generation toward better community health.

The GROW model is a well-respected coaching framework that helps guide these conversations[152], as it focuses on the manager asking open-ended questions to invoke thoughtful responses. This can help managers begin to shift their approach away from telling others their perspective, and instead invite the discussion and perspective of their team members. The approach aligns directly with the creation of psychological safety, as it invites a conversation instead of simply providing answers.

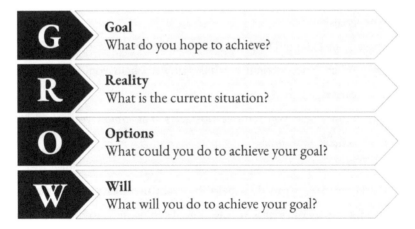

Figure 10: The GROW coaching model uses open-ended questions to help team members arrive at a plan to support goal achievement.

To help ensure a shared understanding of the intent of the conversation, begin a coaching session by establishing the topic you'll cover. Let's consider a career conversation a manager might have with a team member, where she asks the following questions that are aligned to GROW.

(Goal) The manager will start by understanding the team member's goal.

- What do you hope to achieve in your career?
- What is career success for you?
- What imagery do you see when you think of your successful career?

(Reality) She will then understand the current situation.

- What previous successes can you use to help you achieve your career goals?
- What is currently holding you back from achieving your career goals?
- How does your current role help to position you for your future goals?

(Options) She can then help the team member consider options.

- What actions could you take now to help you achieve your career goals?
- How could you remove obstacles that inhibit your ability to achieve your goals?
- How can others support your journey to achieve your goals?

(Will) The manager can then help the team member create a plan to move forward. Consider S.M.A.R.T. goal setting here, to help the team member create a plan that is Specific, Measurable, Assignable, Realistic, and Time-related. Like we did for our team goals, also consider why the team member wants to pursue the career goal.

- What action will you take in the next month to help you achieve your goal?

- How will you know if you're making progress toward your goal?
- What is your primary motivation to achieve your goal, your "why?"

A successful GROW coaching discussion will result in the manager only asking open-ended questions that help the team member arrive at their own decisions, without observations, feedback, or affirmation from the facilitator. Based on what I've seen across many managers at Google, the focus on questioning can initially feel uncomfortable, especially in a work culture that often asks managers to provide their perspective, feedback, and advice.

I was admittedly initially skeptical of this approach, and it took me a lot of practice to feel I could approach GROW coaching in a way that felt genuine and helpful. All of that practice led to an epiphany. When I approach a coaching discussion with genuine curiosity, not with a desire to impose my view, the team member gains the benefit of being able to express their thoughts openly and freely. They can explore their own interests and pursuits without my inputs, removing my biases from the discussion. Most individuals can identify their own perspectives and goals and, if given the space to reflect and share, can uncover them in a coaching meeting. All of this directly supports psychological safety through reflection and open dialogue, in a supportive environment.

Gareth Chick is the Founder of Collaborative Equity and a leader in GROW training. He's identified a few habits for managers to recognize and practice avoiding during coaching sessions. He refers to these as (O)ur (U)nconscious (C)ontrolling (H)abits (OUCH!)[153]. Each habit reminder is intended to help the manager remain focused on open-ended questions while not imposing their thoughts on the team member. These are the most common challenges exhibited by managers in coaching situations.

Closed-ended Questions: Closed-ended questions have limited response options, like "yes," "no," or selection of an answer from a list. They limit the learner's options for answering and typically lack the ability to encourage thoughtful reflection. When phrased without expectation, open-ended questions require the learner to form their own perspective and provide a free-form answer, uninhibited by an expectation or specific answer options. Open-ended questions inspire reflection and thoughtful consideration, which is the intent of coaching. Questions that start with "what" or "how" are often the most effective in supporting reflection. We'll continue the example conversation.

When a manager asks a closed-ended question like, "Do you want to be a manager sometime in your career?" she has already anchored the team member in the idea of becoming a manager. If the team member responds to what has been asked and doesn't elaborate, the manager is stuck with an answer of "yes," "no," or "maybe." Little has been gained by the manager or the team member.

If she instead asks an open-ended question like, "What imagery do you see when you think of your successful career?" the team member will usually pause to consider what a successful career might be for them. And then, they will create an image of what that success could look like. Both steps help to inspire a discussion that wouldn't be immediately possible with the closed-ended question. The manager can continue this thoughtful consideration by continuing to ask more open-ended questions.

Filling Silences: As stated, when the manager has asked a good open-ended question intended to inspire reflection, her team member usually needs time to think before they can respond. This silence can feel uncomfortable, but it serves two purposes.

First, the silence allows the team member the space to consider their answer, which can feel even more important for someone who identifies as introverted.[154] A five second pause might feel long to the manager, but it could be exactly what the team member needs to gather their thoughts.

Second, the silence ensures the manager doesn't introduce bias into the team member's response. She might feel a need to motivate the team member to provide an answer or share potential answer options to the question she just asked. After asking "What imagery do you see when you think of your successful career?" she could easily fill a silence with potential answers like "become a manager," "move to your favorite city," or "earn a larger salary." Each of these answers introduces ideas that might not align with what the team member planned to share, but they now might feel compelled to explore the topics the manager introduced. It's best to avoid these prompts and allow the team member to explore their own options.

Multiple Inputs: If a manager asks multiple questions in a row, the team member is most likely to answer the question that is easiest, or the one the manager asked last. Asking a single question will ensure focus on the topic that the manager and team member hope to explore.

The GROW approach to coaching is only effective if the manager is genuine, trying to help the team member consider new and alternative approaches through open-ended questions. It requires a situation that has potential to change, and a manager that is truly curious.

If the manager already knows the answer she wants to hear, or if the company requires an approach to achieve an outcome, coaching won't be appropriate. Instead, the manager should provide feedback and more direct guidance. Working with regulatory compliance is an example where coaching is unlikely to be helpful. If the government or industry requires specific processes for legal compliance, it would be a waste of time for the manager to ask questions and encourage reflection. Instead, she would better serve the team by providing feedback to support prescribed compliance.

Coaching is also only effective if the manager is genuinely curious and truly listening to the answers she receives. As we learned earlier, managers can create psychological safety by listening. When they feel safe, the team member is more comfortable sharing honest responses and exploring new alternatives, without fear of judgment. When done well, coaching can provide a direct and positive impact on the team's feelings of psychological safety.

In what situations can coaching provide a better outcome than feedback?

What opportunities will you pursue in the next week to coach?

Demonstrate Best Practices—Modeling Behavior

In addition to feedback and coaching, modeling behavior can also help to promote ongoing open discussions within a team. This approach is particularly valuable for creating psychological safety because it often requires the manager to be vulnerable, with the team able to see her expertise alongside skill areas that need improvement. I would typically model behavior in moments where my team had less experience, like a high-stakes sales pitch, meeting with Google leadership, or where we needed to respond to a uniquely difficult work situation. But we also used this approach for general skill development. Modeling can occur during a mock practice session or the actual event, with the expectation that the team member will then use the skills they learn in the next meeting or difficult situation.

Mock Session

Mock sessions can include feedback, coaching, and the demonstration of best practices. They're designed to replicate the expected experience of an upcoming real meeting or conversation, allowing the manager and team member to role play what they might encounter. The manager and team member play active roles within the session, each with clear expectations of the other. These can be playful or intended to mimic the level of stress expected in the meeting.

I led a playful mock session early in my sales management career, where I hoped to help recent college graduates understand how to create an effective sales pitch. Some of the team members were feeling pressure to simultaneously understand the application for all of Google's advertising products and how to present effectively to a room of customer decision makers. The complexity of Google's products can be daunting, especially early in a Google seller's career, and it can be intimidating to present to a group of senior decision makers. Combined, these challenges can feel stifling.

So, I removed the barriers created by work and created a mock session that felt more fun than a traditional preparation meeting. I asked the team to choose something they love and create a presentation to tell me why I should also love it. The goal was to practice how to effectively convey a message and create alignment across a group. One of the most memorable was a woman on my team who shared why I should also love *Harry Potter* books.

She created a presentation about why *Harry Potter* was great, including an introduction about the books and an overview of the characters. She felt no pressure pitching *Harry Potter* because there was very little risk of failure. If I left the discussion unconvinced about the joy *Harry Potter* books might bring me, we could laugh about it and move on. The presentation also gave us the opportunity to discuss the basis for any good sales pitch—how the thing she was selling related to my interests and goals. *Harry Potter's* story background and character development are fairly uninteresting to me unless they align to my interests, just as Google advertising products are likely uninteresting to a customer if they don't support their goals.

Through this discussion I celebrated her moments of brilliance, explaining why and how her approach would also work well with customers. I also modeled alternative approaches to drive better alignment with customers, presenting new ways to connect *Harry Potter* to her audience. By the end of the session, she had practiced her pitch and saw me demonstrate alternative approaches to the same conversation. She considered what felt genuine to her from my approach, learned to focus more on the audiences' goals, and left the mock session with increased confidence to lead her next presentation.

Mock sessions also work for meeting preparation where you want to mimic a more stressful meeting environment. While overseeing our global sales operations enablement team, a team member was going to lead an annual review and planning session with our Vice President. He had the skills and ability to lead the meeting, but we still practiced his delivery to build his confidence. We started with a meeting to align on an approach that felt comfortable for both of us, where we agreed he would lead the process and bring me along the journey. We then met weekly to discuss progress, brainstorm ideas, iterate on a presentation, and practice the delivery. At each step I shared feedback and coached or modeled best practices, depending on the need. Most of my modeling occurred when we met to practice the delivery, as I helped him feel more comfortable adjusting his story flow to the discussion occurring in the meeting, not simply adhering to the slides in a presentation.

Throughout our practice sessions, I'd have him pause so I could provide an alternative delivery approach. I'd then have him immediately practice again, so he could emulate the best practice. Through these mock sessions he learned to create a clear storyline aligned to the Vice President's primary interests, succinctly articulate the most important takeaways, comfortably invite questions, and adjust the presentation to serve the Vice President's needs in the moment.

In the meeting with the Vice President, he delivered nearly flawlessly, focusing on the topics top of mind for our senior leader and adjusting comfortably in the moment, even when the conversation veered away from the original presentation. The Vice President invited him to join a subsequent meeting with his leadership group, and at least partly because of these interactions, the team member was promoted in the next review cycle.

Lead a Challenging Meeting

Another way to demonstrate best practices is by leading a portion or all of a meeting, with the team joining to observe and learn. Compared to mock sessions, where the manager and team member collaborate closely in a practice situation to prepare for something in the future, leading a meeting while others observe can cause the manager to feel more vulnerable. The team expects to see the manager model best practices, but no manager is perfect. So, the team will inevitably observe flaws in addition to expertise.

Imagine a team manager Maya, who will lead a meeting with four senior leaders who oversee large sales teams, and who are responsible for decision-making that impacts a large group of sellers. The intent of the meeting is to align on travel budget allocations across teams for the next year. There is a limited budget to be allocated across the sales teams. Despite a few previous planning sessions with the leaders, each enters this meeting with a different goal and desired outcome. Each also has the same decision-making power as the others, with no single person able to make the decision for everyone else.

Maya must lead the meeting toward a final decision, although she doesn't have decision-making power and is a lower rank than those in the room. She also has the added pressure that her team is watching. This is a great opportunity for Maya to demonstrate her leadership skills. She has the ability to listen to the preferences of others, align leadership around decision-making principles, ask open ended questions to identify shared interests across decision makers, and guide the group toward a decision.

If Maya succeeds, the senior leaders will leave the meeting with an agreement to use the budgets. If she fails, they might need to meet again or escalate the decision to a more senior decision maker. Both outcomes provide learning opportunities for Maya and her team.

She can then have a post-meeting discussion with her team, where the members have the opportunity to provide feedback to their manager. They can share what Maya did well and where she could do better. This is also a great chance to ask questions and schedule follow up mock sessions, if there are skills the team members want to learn before their next meeting.

I've modeled how to run hundreds of sales and enablement meetings with Google Ads customers and senior Google stakeholders. While I've developed expertise and refined my approach over time to achieve consistently positive results, I'm under no delusions that I'm an expert. Every meeting is an opportunity to not only demonstrate best practices I'm confident with, but to learn from the presentation experience so I can continually improve. I could sometimes feel intimidated, especially if I was modeling an approach where I wasn't fully confident yet, or if I knew the meeting outcome was high stakes.

Respond to a Difficult Situation

Managers and their teams can feel many stressful situations at work. These stressors could show up as an unachievable sales target, a difficult stakeholder relationship, a missed promotion opportunity, or an overwhelming workload that requires significant overtime to complete. In these moments we have a choice of how to respond, where the manager can model a healthy approach that expands the space for psychological safety. We explored this leadership tactic when we considered how to set goals aligned to purpose and create the path forward, and it's worth exploring further here.

Situation	Response that Inhibits Psychological Safety	Response that Supports Psychological Safety
Unachievable sales target	Manager complains to her leadership and her team, says the targets are unfair, and reluctantly tries to achieve them	Manager shares her concern with leadership and the team, and then leads discussions to identify new ways to achieve the target
Difficult stakeholder relationship	Manager labels the stakeholder as a problem and avoids meeting with them	Manager recognizes the difficulty and proactively pursues a resolution, inviting the stakeholder to share their perspective and consider approaches to support a mutually beneficial ongoing relationship
Missed promotion opportunity	Manager feels bad for herself, unfavorably comparing her performance to peers who were promoted	Manager asks her leadership and team for feedback about how she can improve, and meets with her promoted peers to learn from them
Overwhelming workload requiring overtime	Manager feels frustrated and mistreated for having to work long hours, but she continues to just get the work done	Manager discusses the long hours with her leadership and team, sharing the burden she is feeling and asks for advice to reduce the workload

Figure 11: The manager's response to a difficult situation is an opportunity to model psychological safety.

If the manager responds poorly to challenging situations, the stress she feels can spread through the team like an emotional contagion, negatively impacting team performance and business results. Consider some response options for a manager experiencing the difficulties described above.

The manager who supports psychological safety through a difficult experience will speak openly about her experience, ask others for advice, and adjust her approach to support success for herself and her team. In each of these scenarios, the manager has the opportunity to show vulnerability and strength by asking for help, which sets the stage for her team members to feel psychologically safe to speak up when they experience similar challenges. These difficult moments provide a significant opportunity to personally grow and to positively influence those around us, resulting in better business results from the learning we gain along the way.

What skill is most important to develop to be successful in your role? How can you create a playful mock session to practice this skill?

What opportunity do you have to lead a meeting and collect feedback in the next month?

How do you currently respond to difficult work situations? What steps can you take to respond in a way that supports psychological safety?

PART FOUR:

Cultural Impact—

Influence Psychological Safety Across Your Organization

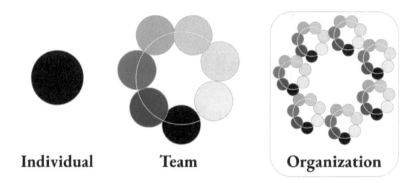

Individual   **Team**   **Organization**

We've now considered how we can begin to create psychological safety for ourselves and integrate it into the work we do with our teams. We have significant control over how we respond to our individual situations and we can influence feelings of psychological safety within our teams.

Shifting organizational culture to embrace psychological safety will be a more difficult task.

Timothy Clark, founder of LeaderFactor and a leader in psychological safety explains why this organizational shift is so difficult. We might be able to change workplace structures and procedures with relative ease, if the right leadership is in place. And these procedural changes might even cause team leader and member behavioral change when someone is watching … or if we are required to be compliant. But the culture of an organization does not truly change until we align with the beliefs and values of the employees[155].

If we want to create lasting and rewarding change that expands beyond basic compliance, we have to create the conditions that encourage and reward those who take the personal risk of engaging in psychologically safe behaviors beyond their working teams. This is particularly challenging when we recognize most of us have less control over what happens across our organization.

Many of us might feel we have no chance of impacting our company's culture. And this might be true, at least in the short term. It might feel overwhelming to shift the mindset of the company leader and executive team so they all genuinely embrace and espouse psychological safety for their employees. And even when the leadership does embrace it, like Google has historically, it's easy to assume we can't make a difference at a company with nearly 190,000 employees[156].

When we try to influence the mentality of a large group of people we move away from the control of our individual psychological safety and into the realm of uncertain impact. So, it can help to start with appropriate expectations. On average, any company-wide change will take longer, require more approvals, and have a higher failure rate than any change we control for ourselves. But in the rare situations where we can successfully make a company-wide change, we have the potential to create a big impact.

As with most decisions about how we dedicate our effort at work, there are tradeoffs to working toward change. Each of us has finite time in our days. So, when we dedicate time to one thing, we automatically forgo another action we could be taking. But we make these decisions about tradeoffs every day, often without noticing. There is no universally correct approach to where we focus our efforts, as each provides different benefits to ourselves and others.

We can feel rewarded, happier, and drive better business results at each stage of psychological safety development. We might want to simultaneously have high control over outcomes and have significant impact for the organization, but high control and organizational impact can sometimes feel at odds with each other. Typically, as the audience size grows our control decreases ... but our breadth of impact increases, and vice-versa (Figure 12). Each of us will need to find the balance that feels appropriate for ourselves, teams, and companies.

I found the best balance of control and impact by considering psychological safety in all of my personal and team interactions, finding ways to provide space for open communication in every situation. I then dedicated a smaller portion of my time, approximately 10 percent, to trying to influence larger teams and company culture.

How will you allocate your effort to yourself, team, or organization?

Figure 12: Control and impact are often inversely related, with our ability to control outcomes declining as the potential breadth of our impact increases.

Before moving forward, I'll pause for a reminder of something that is obvious but might be easy to forget. Your company's leadership is human.

I've seen many examples, within Google and across media, where people without context or full understanding pass significant judgment on decisions made by company leaders. When we have limited interactions with these leaders, and when we lack the full context on which they base their decisions, it can become easy to speculate, judge, and label them as "bad" or "good."

I invite everyone to lead cultural changes with empathy, acknowledging that company leaders are also human. They'll have moments of greatness and moments of failure. A culture of psychological safety provides the opportunity for changemakers to reflect on these moments and support improvement, with the same grace and care we would hope leadership would grant to us.

CHAPTER 10:
GIVE A VOICE TO ALL

Crowdsourcing is a way of collecting input from a large group of people, which helps fund new companies, provide services, and improve existing companies.

Crowdsource Input

If you have a creative idea but lack funding you might turn to Kickstarter, a crowdfunding site that brings creative projects to life. Instead of allowing elite executives to define our culture, Kickstarter provides a connection between creators and a global community of potential investors. Since the company started in 2009, 22 million people have contributed more than $7 billion to 240 thousand funded creative projects. Kickstarter has helped creators launch new comics, an engine-building game, ethically and sustainably sourced mini chocolate bars, an AI-powered pen, and many other products[157]. Their success is only possible because Kickstarter has enabled an open connection between people to share ideas and funding.

Airbnb is another company that relies on crowdsourcing. It all started in 2007; Brian Chesky and Joe Gebbia were struggling to pay their rent when they heard that a conference coming to San Francisco had filled all available hotel rooms. So, they invited three strangers to stay in their apartment on air mattresses during the conference for a nominal fee. Brian and Joe were able to make some money while forming new friendships with their guests. They realized they might have a new creative business idea, so they partnered with Nathan Blecharczk to found Airbnb. They have since grown to 6.6 million active global listings across 100 thousand cities, allowing for 1.4 billion guests to enjoy vacations in other people's homes. Each of the more than 4 million Airbnb hosts have voluntarily added their homes for rent, earning them more than $180 billion[158].

But crowdsourcing is not limited to recently established tech companies. Any company can learn from the collective wisdom of the crowds.

Founded in 1932, LEGO is an abbreviation of two Danish words that mean "play well," and this is still the company's ideal. In a world that feels as if it is often dominated by technology and the newest trends, LEGO has remained relevant and continues to grow revenue[159]. In fact, LEGO was one of a few toy companies that grew significantly during the COVID-19 pandemic, with $8 billion in sales in 2021, up 27 percent from the year before[160]. While much of this growth is driven by branded kits, the company also engages their customers in a unique way. Anyone can share a design idea for a new LEGO concept, known as LEGO Ideas[161], and others can then vote for the design ideas they want to see available to build. If an idea receives more than 10 thousand supporters, LEGO experts will review it and consider producing it for sale in stores. In the 12 years since the start of LEGO Ideas, customers have designed nearly 50 LEGO kits that have made it to production[162]! Each of these

LEGO Ideas winners receives 10 complimentary copies of the set and 1 percent of total net sales of the product. LEGO has found a way to build a relationship with passionate customers to collect and market new ideas and expand on their product line, while also rewarding their customers for their efforts.

Effective crowdsourcing is not a free-for-all. Kickstarter, Airbnb, and LEGO have requirements for engagement, each relying on their community to engage honestly. Just like psychological safety, crowdsourcing relies on trust in order to provide benefit to the community. Among other requirements, Kickstarter projects must be honest on their representation of the product and any related statistics. They do not allow altered videos or imagery to represent something the designer hopes to create in the future; only representation of the actual current version[163]. Airbnb requires hosts to honestly and accurately describe the booking details, location, property type, and amenities[164]. They also confirm guest identities and analyze risk factors of parties in support of their hosts[165]. LEGO Ideas requires designers to adhere to their values, including no sets that represent politics, religion, sex, drugs, horror, shooting, warfare, or bullying[166].

Each of these examples shows how listening to a collective voice can benefit a company, but perhaps more importantly for long-term growth, how that company can continue to be relevant to and benefit their community of customers. Kickstarter connects creators with funders. Airbnb empowers hosts to make money while providing a more home-like feel for travelers. LEGO asks their customers what products they want, and then asks them to establish interest from others through supporting votes. Each company creates the conditions for global input into how their company operates, with a desire to create a better outcome for customers and company.

This same approach of crowdsourcing works for companies to collect feedback and ideas from their employees, in service of improved operations, business performance, and employee happiness!

Imagine a company the size of Google, with nearly 200 thousand employees at the start of 2023. Even a very well-intended and informed executive team is unable to understand the daily jobs and challenges experienced by their employees, unless they make a deliberate effort. The executives are able to maintain their higher-level perspective and guide the company toward future goals, but much of that success is only possible with the collective effort of the 200 thousand individuals who comprise the whole organization. Executives are better able to identify challenges to fix and successes to expand on when they ask their people what they are experiencing.

Google executives recognized the need for crowdsourcing feedback only six years after it was founded, so they launched Googlegeist in 2004[167].

Googlegeist is an anonymous company-wide survey that allows every employee to share feedback and speak up with ideas with no fear of repercussions. Through the survey, leadership collects feedback from employees about their work, managers, leadership, happiness, compensation, inclusion, and many other things associated with our ability to bring our full selves to work. While the survey isn't perfect and can draw skepticism from some employees, nearly 90 percent of Googlers complete the survey every year, providing an overview of sentiment toward the company and its areas that need improvement.

Google leadership seriously considers the Googlegeist outputs, with each manager, Director, Vice President, and C-level executive reviewing the aggregate feedback and written comments. They then share and focus discussion on the main takeaways, including the areas where the company is supporting employees well and the areas they can continue to improve upon. With millions of data points and hundreds of thousands of requests for change, the company leadership can't fix every challenge they hear about, but they can clearly outline priority efforts and rationale for selecting those efforts. In recent years, these discussions have included how to appropriately address disparate feelings of individual inclusion at Google, compensation adjustments to remain competitive, performance management improvements, and remote versus in-office work, among other important areas of concern. For each of these priority initiatives, Google leadership shares what actions they will take and then regularly reports the company's progress.

Amazon appears to run similar surveys for their employees. Amazon Connections is a short daily survey that helps the Human Resources team understand employee experiences, with the goal of helping to "develop leaders who earn trust, remove barriers to excellence and make Amazon an inspiring place to work.[168]" They also share an annual Tech Survey, which asks some comparable questions as Googlegeist[169]. Amazon tech leadership reviews these results and advocates for improvements based on the needs they hear from employees.

Like the crowdsourcing for Kickstarter, Airbnb, and LEGO, Google and Amazon proactively pursue the collective wisdom of the crowds. Their company-wide surveys give a voice to those who might otherwise feel under-represented, allowing everyone to share their perspective and experience. When a company's leadership hears these perspectives, they can work toward improved working conditions that help their employees thrive and that support the company's success. If the company's leadership fails to address genuine concerns, they risk losing great employees and creating a less engaged workforce. When employees offer honest feedback in support of ongoing improvement and leadership genuinely listens and considers how they can make those improvements, these surveys can further reinforce psychological safety across the company.

How does your company currently collect feedback from employees?

What steps can your company take to better listen to employee feedback?

Empower Underrepresented Voices

We can also positively influence psychological safety with initiatives that expand beyond our teams, but perhaps not companywide. I shared *Relate* in Chapter 2, where our leadership team and I listened to the challenges felt by members of underrepresented groups within our individual teams. Our effort started small but then expanded to reach several hundred individuals across multiple countries. By helping to give a voice to those within our teams, we fostered an environment for ongoing improvement.

I also kicked off initiatives to directly improve psychological safety across my last working group and co-led an initiative to help expand networks to historically underrepresented professional talent pools. Both of these projects had an impact beyond my direct working team, supporting hundreds of individuals in sharing their voice in a way they wouldn't have otherwise.

When I first joined Google's enablement team, our group reported some of the lowest psychological safety scores I had seen on Googlegeist. Many of the nearly 150 team members felt uncomfortable sharing ideas or challenging leadership because they perceived both as a risk to their personal development and performance reviews. As a result, our leadership group failed to collect really meaningful feedback and learn from all of our great team members who saw opportunities to improve our operations and delivery.

In my first months on the team I shared this fear of speaking up, so I kept my ideas for improvement to myself. It wasn't until my manager, a wonderful leader who inspires psychological safety for those around her[170], asked me what was holding me back. She asked open-ended questions to uncover my concerns, listened closely to my responses, and then encouraged me to share my perspectives with our Vice President. My manager assured me the team's fear was misguided, and the VP was actually craving the partnership and ideas to improve the team culture.

With my confidence bolstered, I called our VP a few minutes later, shared my apprehension for discussing my ideas with her and asked if she would be open to meeting. The next 20 minutes alleviated my initial fears and resulted in a great conversation about next steps. She invited me to share ideas with her and I brought her a proposal a few days later.

After aligning with the VP on an approach, I organized a meeting where all enablement managers and leadership met bi-weekly. This meeting had existed previously, but we rarely accomplished anything meaningful because those of us not on the executive team didn't feel empowered to speak up. We hoped the new meeting would be different. To support better safety, I also created a manager working group to align on how we can best support our teams and coordinate meetings for the subsequent year to work through the challenges we faced. Our efforts were appropriately called *Belonging*, with our primary intention of helping all 150 members of the enablement team feel an increased sense of belonging, ultimately leading to psychological safety to share their ideas.

Our working group was happy to see significant improvements in our next set of Googlegeist results. One year later, more members felt like they were part of a team where their voices were heard, and they were comfortable speaking up. We undoubtedly still had room to improve though, so we transitioned the work to a new set of managers who could bring their fresh perspectives. They continued the *Belonging* work with new approaches and ideas to further the enablement team's journey toward psychological safety.

I was bolstered by a great manager who encouraged me to speak up the first time, and that cascaded into the ongoing *Belonging* discussions. If you are feeling a concern about speaking up for the good of the broader team, who can you trust to initially talk to and begin building your confidence? While I do not expect all outcomes to mimic mine, I have found that a bit of support and bolstered confidence can provide a great impetus to continue a conversation and hopefully promote more safety over time.

In addition to *Relate* and *Belonging*, I also kicked off and co-led what I believe was Google's first at-scale effort to expand professional networks outside of Google, working alongside my great colleague, Antonio[171]. *The Connections Project* was intended to expand on Google's diversity, equity, and inclusion efforts by directly countering one of the largest challenges to an inclusive hiring process–relying on limited professional networks for candidate sourcing.

Each of us is predisposed to having networks of similar racial, socio-economic, and belief backgrounds[172], with Black people more likely to have smaller networks than Whites[173]. In addition, most jobs are filled from our networks[174] without first being publicly published [175]. In Chapter 6, I shared an eye-opening conversation during a book club, where a woman on my team called me out for not recognizing my privilege. These facts about network entitlement reinforce her comment that I have been able to achieve success in my career without focusing on networking, at least in part, because I am White.

In 2022, more than 90 percent of Google jobs in the US were held by individuals who identified as White or Asian[176]. If most of our networks look like us, and if most hiring comes from our networks, that means Google was more likely to continue its trend of hiring White and Asian candidates into perpetuity. But we chose to break the trend. We wanted to build awareness of this challenge in order to support a more diverse workforce and to directly address representation inequities.

This background was the impetus for us to pursue *The Connections Project*, a US-based initiative. For nearly a year, Antonio and I developed an approach to connect managers within our sales operations organization with professionals who have historically lacked representation in the available talent pool. The effort during that year included the development of our communications strategy, clear expectation setting for Google leadership and the external talent pool that the initiative is for networking (not an immediate hiring initiative), goal setting for the program, surveys to track progress toward the goals, and significant legal reviews before launch approval.

The Connections Project resulted in dozens of networking connections that wouldn't have otherwise existed. We learned from the initial launch, identified ways to improve, and explored opportunities to expand the initiative to Europe. Similar to *Belonging*, the co-lead and I then passed ownership for the project to another set of leads after the first year, so they could expand and improve with new ideas. The project had the potential to impact hundreds of Google managers and their networks, so our project team then integrated the approach into a broader external networking strategy across Google.

Relate, *Belonging*, and *The Connections Project* are examples of how we can begin to expand open dialogue across larger groups. Each was designed in response to a challenge, requiring psychological safety and vulnerability to collaborate across groups to continue a journey of improvement. None of these projects solved all of the problems they set out to fix, but each made progress and provided learning opportunities for the next initiative to perform even better.

Crowdsourcing employee feedback is a great way to understand the success and challenges felt across an organization, so leadership can adjust as needed to achieve the organization's goals. Initiatives like *Relate, Belonging,* and *The Connections Project* can collect feedback from smaller portions of the organization, in support of ongoing growth of psychological safety across larger groups. *Relate* introduced a new way for teams to consider solutions to the issues and identity characteristics that most directly impact team members. *Belonging* helped to directly improve psychological safety concerns across a large team. *The Connections Project* created relationships where they wouldn't have existed otherwise. Each initiative only worked because there was a space to share ideas and discuss challenges, without fear of repercussion. In combination, they can begin to shift company culture to help employees feel empowered to speak up, in favor of improved happiness and performance.

What challenges does your company face? For those challenges that you would like to help solve, how can you start the conversation?

What steps can you take in the next three months to test improvements within and beyond your working team? How can these improvements extend to the broader organization?

CHAPTER 11:
EMBRACE DIFFERENCES

Earlier in this book we reflected on how each of us experiences psychological safety differently, based on our race, gender, sexual orientation, sexual identity, sexual preference, political leanings, and birthplace. Each of these identifiers impacts our feelings of psychological safety and contributes to our biases.

It was likely easier for me to feel psychologically safe as a leader at Google, since 62 percent of Google leaders in the US were White when I left the company, and 70 percent were male. I was also likely in the majority by identifying as heterosexual[177] and cisgender[178]. Based on what I know about Google's compensation, can read on LinkedIn, and have seen in the leadership's communication, I speculate that Google's leadership is more likely to be wealthier, have an advanced education, lean politically liberal, and be born in the US.

If we compare me against Google's leadership, we can see significant overlap in our experience and perspectives, which is more likely to inspire psychological safety in my interactions. We can immediately connect through shared experiences, which can inspire trust.

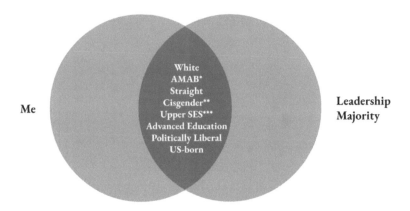

Figure 13: My background and identity overlapped significantly with the majority of Google management in the US at the time of my departure, which helped me to feel more psychologically safe. *AMAB stands for *assigned male at birth*. **Cisgender describes a person whose gender identity corresponds with the sex registered at birth, not transgender. ***Upper socioeconomic status (SES) describes a person who has more access to financial resources than others.

Compare this to someone who was assigned female at birth, is Black, identifies as gay and transgender, is from a lower income family, and immigrated to the US. We will refer to them as Chantel.

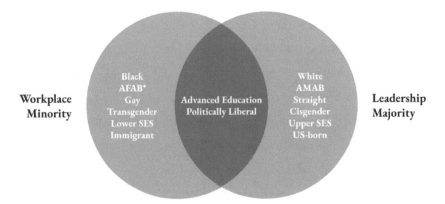

Figure 14: A Google workplace minority shared less background and identity overlap with the majority of Google leadership at the time of my departure, which can make it more difficult to feel psychologically safe. *AFAB stands for assigned female at birth. Note: If Chantel were politically conservative, they would have even fewer areas of overlap with the leadership majority.

I don't intend to focus on myself here, but I'm acknowledging the advantage of those like me in the workplace, as we are more likely to feel safe speaking up in meetings and sharing ideas. Like each of us I have inherent biases, and I also realize we're best equipped to openly explore, embrace, and celebrate diverse perspectives if we first understand our differences.

Each of us is likely at a different stage in our journey of embracing diverse perspectives, so once again, it helps to create a shared language to guide these conversations. Through this shared language, we can discuss our current perspectives and challenge each other to make progress toward more inclusion over time.

Inspired by Milton Bennett's work on intercultural sensitivity[179] and continued studies[180], Dr. Mitchell Hammer created the Intercultural Development Continuum (IDC)[181] to help us consider and shift mindsets from "Monocultural" to "Intercultural." The framework starts at "Denial" and ends at "Adaptation." If we hope to support psychological safety for everyone, we will work to build bridges across diverse communities, striving to reach Adaptation and an Intercultural Mindset.

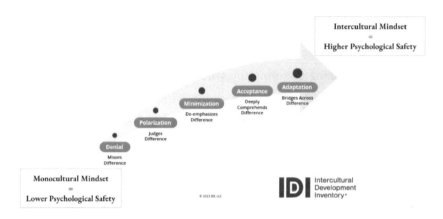

Figure 15: Adapted with approval of the Intercultural Development Inventory. The Intercultural Development Continuum (IDC) framework illustrates the progressive development from a Monocultural Mindset to an Intercultural Mindset. Each step toward Adaptation reflects a deeper embrace of diverse communities, resulting in more open communication aligned to higher psychological safety.

Denial

When we have a Denial mindset, we're not likely to understand or respond appropriately to differences in perspectives, beliefs, responses, or behaviors. Often driven by limited interaction with different cultural groups, we might feel distant from the other cultural groups and therefore stereotype others, due to lack of an understanding of individual perspectives.

At this stage of the continuum, Chantel—being stereotyped—would feel ignored and have low psychological safety.

Polarization

With a "Polarization" mindset we can approach other cultures as "us versus them." Our approach with this mindset is often divisive, comparing cultures as better or worse than each other. Not surprisingly, this can create an uncomfortable work environment. This focus on differences can also result in easier labeling and might create conditions of microaggression, due to a lack of empathy for others' experiences.

At this stage, Chantel and their team would feel uncomfortable discussing diversity and working within a diverse team.

Minimization

"Minimization" is the transition point from a Monocultural Mindset to an Intercultural Mindset, shifting toward a culture of psychological safety. At this point in the continuum, we look for similarities across different cultures and worldviews as we minimize differences, but often at the expense of recognizing important differences and perspectives. This focus on commonalities typically aligns to our basic needs and universal values and principles, which are heavily influenced by the dominant culture groups.

Since Minimization focuses on what we have in common, Chantel might not feel heard when they have an opinion that differs from the team.

Acceptance

"Acceptance" is the first mindset on the continuum that Dr. Hammer would describe as an Intercultural Mindset but is not yet at the level of Adaptation. At the Acceptance stage, we recognize and appreciate the common elements across diverse cultures, along with the differences. We want to learn about the different perspectives around us and reflect on how those perspectives align with ours. We embrace and understand others' views, but we might still struggle to adapt or respond to cultural differences that we consider unethical or immoral.

At this stage, Chantel feels understood.

Adaptation

When we reach an Adaptation mindset, we build on the positive attributes of the previous mindsets along the continuum. We are curious about other perspectives and reflect on how those perspectives differ and align with ours to ensure a feeling of understanding across our teams. But we also shift our perspective based on what we learn. We change our behavior, when appropriate and authentic. As we learn more about and embrace other cultures, we develop the ability to create connections across diverse communities, resulting in our teams feeling valued and involved.

Chantel finally feels valued, involved, and psychologically safe.

While the IDC does not directly address psychological safety, the continuum starts with an insular mindset and ends with a mindset that embraces open communication with ongoing improvement for how we build connections across diverse cultures and viewpoints. When we achieve a team and organizational environment that is filled with Acceptance and Adaptation, we also achieve an environment filled with psychological safety, where diverse communities can come together and share ideas without fear. Just as each member of our team experiences psychological safety differently, each also likely sits at a different stage of the IDC continuum.

Team members who identify with the dominant culture often have the luxury of not having to consider other cultural perspectives to succeed at work. When we identify with the dominant culture, we find it easy to adhere to the established working norms, since those norms align with how we already think and act. I likely benefited from this at Google, while lack of identification with the dominant culture inhibited others. The discrepant benefit allowed to the majority is something we can proactively avoid, if we achieve Acceptance and Adaptation.

Members of a non-dominant culture, typically those who are underrepresented at work like Chantel, are more likely to feel a strain between their perspective and that of the dominant culture around them. In a team environment of Denial, Polarization, and Minimization, the burden often falls to the individuals who identify with non-dominant cultures to assimilate to those around them, instead of being true to themselves. And in situations where members of the dominant culture hope to learn about the non-dominant cultures, the burden often falls on those in the minority to explain their perspectives and teach others. Frameworks like the IDC can help to guide everyone to a shared understanding and open communication in order to reduce the burdens placed on the non-dominant cultures.

With practice, we will find the right balance of embracing differences and similarities in a team run on high psychological safety.

Where do you feel you currently sit within the Intercultural Development Continuum? Where would others say you sit?

What steps can you take in the next three months to move closer to Adaptation?

PART FIVE:

Build the Habit of Psychological Safety

If you don't take action on what you have learned, none of the knowledge in this book matters. Knowledge alone does not result in behavior change. It's simply the starting point toward change. The shift in our behavior comes through repeated attempts to integrate knowledge into our daily lives. One popular learning model estimates only ten percent of our learning occurs through studying things like this book, with ninety percent happening through individual practice and interaction with others[182].

Creating and maintaining psychological safety requires an ongoing commitment to practice. That commitment will reward you with a happier team and improved business results. With no commitment to improve, we will continue our current habits instead of forming new ones and will fail to see the desired change within and beyond ourselves.

CHAPTER 12:
PRACTICE DELIBERATELY

Greylag geese are large for their species, with brownish gray feathers and an orangish beak. A female greylag goose is born with the innate desire to, when she becomes a mother, keep her eggs in her nest. If one of her eggs rolls away, she will instinctively use her beak to roll it back into the nest. This behavior is so hardwired that she'll try to move any nearby egg-shaped object into her nest. Researchers have placed golf balls and volleyballs near a mother goose's nest and observed her trying to roll them home!

It might be comical to imagine a momma bird trying to save a volleyball from the horrors beyond her nest, but we humans are not very different. Our habits can become so ingrained in our behaviors that we sometimes act like a greylag goose, moving a volleyball where an egg should sit. We repeat our habits with very little thought or awareness of the impact on our lives.

Understanding Habit Development

A habit is a learned behavior that we regularly perform with little mental effort or awareness. We briefly referenced the creation of habits when we considered the challenges of learning a new skill in Chapter 4, acknowledging habits fall into the category of our System 1 thinking and our automatic behavior. These are the things we do with very little consciousness or mental effort. While some habits might be ingrained in us, like the greylag goose mom protecting her eggs, many of our habits are the result of repeated practice over time. Some help to make our lives better, like the habit of tooth-brushing I hope my son will soon adopt. Other habits can harm us, like smoking. When we recognize our habits relative to what we hope to achieve, we can deliberately change existing habits and create new behaviors.

With practice, each of us can create the habit of activating psychological safety at work.

During my time leading Google's enablement teams, I dedicated nearly two years studying behavior change and meeting with habit development experts. I've reviewed multiple theories across psychology and within academia and popular culture about how we can create positive habits in our lives and transition away from our harmful habits.

The origin for much of what we pursue for habit change seems to have been influenced by cognitive behavior therapy (CBT). Aaron Beck was a professor at the University of Pennsylvania and developed CBT in the 1960s[183.] He spent his 70-year career trying to stop human suffering. More than 2,000 clinical trials since its development have shown CBT to help people alleviate psychological and physical challenges[184].

Dr. Beck recognized that our interpretations of a situation influence our emotional and behavioral responses more than the actual situation. Our interpretations of situations are sometimes distorted, based on our underlying beliefs. Someone who often feels depressed might distort situations in a way that makes them err toward seeing situations as negative or harmful, due to underlying beliefs aligned to loss or failure. Those of us who tend to feel optimism also distort situations, just in a way that makes us view them more positively.

Consider a situation where I lead a meeting with a customer who is essential to my team and my manager's success. My manager is unable to join and she sends an email at 10:00 p.m. that only says, "What happened at the meeting?" I glance at my email as I get into bed to go to sleep, and my mind immediately begins to swirl with automatic thoughts. I think of all the things that could have gone wrong, what my manager might have heard, and why she might have emailed me so late at night. I focus on potential things that my team or I could have messed up, and I stay awake thinking about how to address these in the morning. First thing in the morning, I rush to my manager's office to learn what's wrong, only to hear she was simply curious and trying to show interest. She had no judgment or concerns about the meeting. I worried and stayed awake simply because of my misinterpretation of a well-intentioned, curious email.

Like habits, these interpretations are often automatic and occur without conscious thought. They impact our emotions, physiological response, and actions.

CBT prompts us to recognize when we are responding to our interpretations to a situation, and not to the situation itself. Dr. Judith Beck of the Beck Institute, the daughter of Aaron Beck and also a leader in CBT, would have encouraged me to recognize my negative thoughts and question my thinking about my manager's email[185.] If I had paused to consider my manager's perspective and our historically positive relationship, I might have come to an alternative conclusion—that she is a caring leader who was simply curious about my meeting. I could have let go of the worry and had a good night's sleep!

My example manager email is a simplified version of how CBT works. If we begin to recognize the situations in which we hope to respond differently, we can identify the current thoughts we have in those situations and consider alternatives. If we practice these alternative thoughts over time, with a focus on making incremental daily improvements, we can begin to shift our responses to situations.

Similar steps show up in most habit-change research, hinting that CBT's approach extends beyond the treatment of conditions like anxiety or depression, and into our everyday habits. Thousands of peer reviewed studies over more than 50 years have shown CBT's effectiveness, so we can also be confident in its ability to support our habit development. I have simplified the approach to three components.

1. Understand how our habits work.
2. Practice what we hope to create as a habit, preferably emulating best practices.
3. Repeat practice over time, acknowledging small gains can have big impacts.

Fortunately, we can change our habits. Once we understand the situations that cause us to take an action, we can identify alternative actions and practice a new routine. We can shift our habits by altering what Pulitzer-prize winner and best-selling author Charles Duhigg calls the cue, routine, or our reward[186].

What habit in your life would you most like to change?

In what situations do you demonstrate the habit? What action do you take? How do you feel after?

Practice

Let's say the habit I want to change is the excessive time I spend on social media. If I hope to break an unhealthy social media habit but still engage with my friends online, I might want to continue using some social media with intention but eliminate the unconscious habit. I assume I can keep my social media accounts, since they are a great way for me to connect with friends and family, particularly those who don't live nearby.

Adjusting my behavior trigger—or cue—would be the easiest way to change my social media habit. I could simply turn off notifications, but this alone would be unlikely to change my behavior. It might support a reduction in social media use due to fewer reminders, but I would still feel the urge to check the status of my latest post. I would continue to check sites, even in the absence of the notifications.

If I keep my notifications on, I could change how I respond by replacing my current response to the notification with something new. Instead of immediately checking my phone after I hear the notification, I could instead rub my index finger with my thumb until the craving passes. This might sound goofy, but the alternative simple action could help to break the cycle of immediately grabbing my phone.

I could also document how eliminating my cue (turning notifications off) or enacting a different response to the cue (rubbing my fingers) impacted how I felt. My reward would change with a reduction in social media use. I might enjoy exiting the rollercoaster of emotion caused by monitoring responses to my most recent post and begin to feel happier spending less time viewing social media.

Once we identify the changes to our cues and routines that result in the largest desired impact, we can then focus our energy to practice developing the new habit. Replacing my social media checking routine with rubbing my fingers could require many months of daily practice, but the reward of improved happiness would be worth the effort!

We can apply the same approach to psychological safety at work.

When was the last time you experienced something challenging at work, but didn't try to fix it? There are a variety of reasons why we might not try to fix a problem we see. We might assume we can't fix it, believe leadership should take care of it, have had a negative experience the last time we spoke up, or just don't have the energy to deal with the additional effort. We might instead complain about the problem to our spouse or friends and continue to deal with the ongoing challenge at work. This can develop a habit of not speaking up at work, with the reward of bonding with friends or family outside of work. But the reward is fleeting and doesn't improve our working conditions.

If we have high psychological safety and a desire to improve our work environment, we can recognize this cue of a problem at work and adjust our response. When we see a problem, we can instead speak up and share ideas to fix it, resulting in improved working conditions and business outcomes. When we have psychological safety, we will feel comfortable discussing the problem, even if we don't know how to fix it or feel we have the energy to fix it ourselves. By starting the conversation, we might identify ideas from other team members or interest from others to solve it. The reward is then ongoing, with future work experiences being better than before.

The manager and leadership will play a key role in inviting this habit development. In the absence of manager support and commitment for improvement, the reward might not support the ongoing sharing of ideas and the team could revert to not sharing. If the manager supports the discussion and brainstorming to solve problems, other members of the team will see the benefits and be more likely to repeat this positive cycle of open communication.

If this routine shift feels daunting, Stanford University professor BJ Fogg's *Tiny Habits*[187] might help get you started. Fogg believes in the power of aligning small behavior changes to existing prompts in our lives. These prompts align with Duhigg's cues, and the routine we pursue can be small to start. If you initially feel uncomfortable or unprepared to discuss a problem and share a solution with your manager, consider starting with something simpler. We might not always have the words to describe a problem we are experiencing or to articulate a solution to those problems. Instead, the team and manager could align on a simple phrase to indicate there's a need for a conversation.

For example, when my team and I were in a brainstorming session, our conversations would often lead us down tangents unrelated to the task at hand. At the start of the brainstorming meetings, we'd identify a fun code word to bring us back on track without feeling we were interrupting our teammates. Borrowed from the Pixar movie *Up*, when the endearing golden retriever character would get distracted by a squirrel and immediately lose focus, we would say "squirrel" whenever we got off topic. This was a lighthearted cue to help us bring the conversation back toward the topic we hoped to discuss.

We could use a similar approach to indicate a need to discuss a problem at work. What code word could you and your team use to indicate the need to discuss a problem at work? How can each of us create a simple approach to help us signal the need for a discussion, even when we don't know how to solve the problem? These efforts can lead to a follow up discussion to help support ongoing improvements. Aligned to the ideas of *Tiny Habits*, this simplified approach can help reduce barriers to habit change, if we find alternatives to be too challenging.

As the team members practice this new routine, with the reward of a better working environment and improved team performance, they will build comfort in sharing ideas. Each reward reinforces others to respond similarly when they identify a challenge to solve, helping each team member build the habit of psychologically safe idea sharing over time. Through repetition, this can then become a habit.

Consider the habit you would like to change.

How could you change the cue that causes you to perform the habit?

What alternative behaviors could you enact, instead of your current habit?

Repeat

We are most likely to develop a habit if we practice a single skill deliberately and repeatedly over time.

There is no magic number of times to practice creating a habit, but researchers from the Cancer Research UK Health Behavior Research Centre debunked the oversimplified belief that we can create new habits in 21 days, finding it took up to nearly nine months to create some habits[188]. Gaining expertise takes even longer. Best-selling author Malcolm Gladwell popularized the idea of 10,000 hours of practice to gain expertise[189]. This assertion builds on studies completed by Herbert

Simon and William Chase, who researched chess masters and grandmasters that spent an estimated 10,000 to 50,000 hours of practice to achieve the pinnacle of their success[190]. Those who are considered the best in their field also had innate talent, access to support from other experts, and privileged conditions surrounding them to support their learning.

Each of us can build a habit of pursuing psychological safety if we commit to practice. I also believe each of us can achieve psychological safety expertise, even without innate talent. We can learn from books like this and other education on the topic, find the conditions in which we feel comfortable practicing and commit to ongoing improvement.

If we strive to practice psychological safety improvements for 10,000 hours, we'd have to dedicate 20 hours every week for nearly ten years. This is important to recognize because the development of psychological safety, like any worthwhile aspiration, is a journey. Throughout that journey, you'll sometimes succeed and create a space of open communication that helps everyone thrive, and you'll also experience setbacks. If you stick with the journey and continually learn with each experience, psychological safety will continue to develop within and around you.

Most of us will succeed in our skill development through incremental gains.

The idea of incremental improvement has recently become increasingly popular, particularly with the idea of getting 1 percent better every day. The theory tells us we can become 37 times better at something after one year of incremental, daily 1 percent improvements. This is a fun way to visualize ongoing improvement and reminds us that we can make big changes with small gains over time. We should temper our expectations though, as we pursue our incremental growth.

This idea of exponential improvement borrows from the concept of compound interest, long a staple of financial planning and ancient wisdom, believed to have been first introduced approximately 4,000 years ago in Babylon[191]. While exponential improvement works well to describe many financial trends over time, it seems a bit foolish to think we could become 37 times better at most meaningful skills in one year. It might feel good to apply a numerical value to skill development, but many skills are very difficult to quantify. This is particularly true for psychological safety, which we know is dependent on the situation and individual experiencing it. Even if we could effectively create a psychological safety score, it'd only be valid in one situation, not on a universal scale. Also, while I'm not aware of any reliable quantifiable data about habit development, the world of finance hints that a 37-fold improvement in one year is an unlikely event.

Consider a real-life money example with the S&P 500. Since 1927, the S&P 500 has tracked the stock performance of the 500 largest companies listed on stock exchanges in the United States[192]. The value of an investment in the S&P 500 would have grown more than 200 times over the last 96 years (Figure 16), an impressive rate of return. But this real-life example highlights three things for us to consider as we pursue our incremental growth through tiny gains.

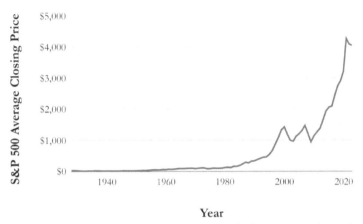

Figure 16: Compounding incremental improvements can lead to exponential growth over time, but this real-life example of the S&P 500 helps to set expectations about how quickly we can improve. We are unlikely to improve 1 percent every day, in perpetuity.

Results are variable. The value of the S&P 500 declined on average one of every three years. We can expect setbacks along our growth journey. If we expect constant improvement, we might feel discouraged when we encounter significant challenges or temporary failures. But these challenges are part of the journey and make us stronger over time!

Growth is slow. It took the S&P 500 sixty-nine years to achieve the same growth (37 times) as the daily 1 percent improvement aspires for us to achieve in one year. Once again, we might feel disappointed if we expect immediate and ongoing daily improvements. When we recognize our skill development will take time, we can grant ourselves patience and enjoy the process, instead of feeling we are always behind.

Growth stagnates. The S&P 500 only includes the largest 500 companies in the United States and this list of companies changes regularly. Twenty-two of the 500 companies are replaced by new companies every year, and the top companies rarely remain at the top for extended periods of time[193]. The same applies to our skills. At some point, our required skill development will change as our environment changes and other aspects of our skill-set plateau.

I temper expectations here to set us up for success. If we know incremental gains are important for us to achieve our long-term goal of creating a psychologically safe workplace, we can proactively recognize and positively respond to the challenges we face along the way.

I am a big proponent of working toward incremental improvements. But I have found it also helps maintain our motivation when we begin with appropriate expectations. As we learn a new skill or continue to improve existing skills, we are more likely to follow the real-world S&P 500 trend, not the mythical ongoing improvement of the 1 percent rule. We can expect to encounter challenges along the way. We might accidentally and temporarily break trust or fail to create a safe space for those around us, causing us to regress temporarily in our progress toward psychological safety.

Just like financial markets, human behavior and progress is difficult (if not impossible) to forecast accurately. We all experience unexpected variables throughout our journeys, which make uninterrupted growth impossible. But with patience and ongoing commitment, we can continue toward our goal of making a habit of building psychologically safe spaces. We will eventually reach a point at which we are no longer conscious of our efforts to build and maintain psychological safety, with our actions feeling automatic.

If we are lucky, we can ultimately create a feeling of flow for us and those around us.

 What is one thing you can practice every day to invite feedback and conversation at work?

CHAPTER 13:
PURSUE FLOW

Of the nearly 60 million people in the United States who participate in running every year, only one in 1,000 will complete an ultra-race. A running event that is longer than the 26.2 miles of a marathon, ultra races can be as long as the 268-mile Montane Spine race along the Pennine Way in Britain. This race is clearly not for the casual runner, with nearly seven miles of elevation gain and up to six and a half days of racing! I love outdoor adventures, but I can't imagine surviving a race like that.

Many ultra runners suffer through muscle and joint injuries, digestive problems, and a sometimes-dangerous decline of sodium in the blood called hyponatremia[194,] which can lead to vomiting, confusion, and weakness. Some ultra runners have even reported hallucinations during these races, seeing severed heads in a water trough, rotisserie chickens hanging in front of them, a lawnmower blocking their path, and a naked woman holding a machine gun behind a bush[195]... none of which actually existed. For any non-runner, and for those of us who have only run up to the marathon distance, these physical and mental impacts might deter us from attempting to run so far.

But ultra runners can also experience many benefits when they overcome the physical and temporary mental challenges. As they push their body and mind to the extreme, they can enhance their health and become sick less often than others[196], improve their cardiovascular and muscular strength and endurance, and—for those who cross the finish line—gain a potentially life-altering positive feeling of achievement.

Many ultra runners also experience something called flow.

Flow

Flow is the "state in which people are so involved in an activity that nothing else seems to matter; the experience itself is so enjoyable that people will do it even at great cost, for the sheer sake of doing it[197]." Psychologist Mihaly Csikszentmihalyi believes flow to be the source of happiness, a life worth living. Through their repeated practice, many running 20 hours per week for a year and usually building on prior years of running experience, ultra runners have created the conditions to tap into human happiness while achieving what most would consider an unattainable goal.

Flow can be difficult to achieve and I don't want to overstate its potential value, but Csikszentmihalyi's arguments are compelling and worth considering.

Csikszentmihalyi lived through World War II before the age of ten and saw the war's impact on the adults around him. After experiencing the horrors of war, with their home and families taken from them, the adults were unable to live a content and happy life. So, he dedicated his life to understanding what leads to a life worth living[198].

After exploring a few options across religion and psychology,

Csikszentmihalyi started to see trends in the experiences that caused happiness for individuals. A trained musician described a moment of ecstasy when they were able to compose music, almost as if he didn't exist and the music poured out of him. A poet described a feeling of floating, where the ideas effortlessly flowed onto the page. An ice skater shared her experience that felt automatic, requiring no thinking, just allowing a merger with the music to complete a skating program that clicked into a well-orchestrated routine. Flow tends to show up at work where there is a balanced desire from leadership for their employees to feel joy as they pursue the company's mission, often with a clear connection to supporting others. Each of us has likely felt these types of moments, when we become immersed in our activity and feel as if our work or play becomes effortless.

We cannot force this feeling of flow. We must simply embrace it as it happens.

Despite not being able to force it, Csikszentmihalyi found some conditions that seem to help people arrive at flow. After collecting more than 8,000 interviews, he found several conditions for flow, all of which transcend cultural differences and economic backgrounds. When we are in flow, we have a singular focus on what we are doing and feel a great sense of clarity that can result in ecstasy, a feeling of being disconnected from our everyday tasks. We gain a sense of serenity, letting go of our ego, allowing ourselves to be fully immersed in the task without concern for time. All of this is inspired by our pursuit of an intrinsically motivated challenge for which we have the skills to achieve.

Ultra runners have clarity around a singular focus of placing one foot in front of the other, helping them to become fully immersed in that task. For many, this can result in a loss of consideration of time as they align their focus toward the intrinsic motivation to complete the race.

We are most likely to achieve flow when we fluctuate between emotional states of arousal and control. When the challenge we are pursuing is slightly beyond our current ability, we become aroused. This is where we learn and grow. This can show up physically for the first-time ultra-runner, or for the tenured runner taking on a more difficult course. Control is where we feel comfortable and can more easily demonstrate our skills. Since we cannot always perform above our current skills, control provides some balance to allow us to continue moving forward with less effort. This might show up for the ultra-runner during a flat portion of the course, where they can simply trust their training and allow their legs to carry them forward.

Flow and Psychological Safety at Work

At this point, you might be curious how flow can apply to psychological safety at work. Sure, this might work for dedicated athletes, writers, and musicians that have the private space, time, and lack of distraction to allow them to get into flow. But how can it work for me during a hectic workday? This is a very reasonable question, and I expect each of us will need to find our own path toward flow at work. I will share my story to hopefully inspire ideas for you to consider.

When I took over leadership of my first sales teams in 2010, I felt a strong need to achieve my sales targets. Although I suspect I was not supposed to know, I learned soon after taking the role that one of the people on my interview panel felt I was too inexperienced to lead a team. Luckily, I had several advocates who convinced them that it was worth giving me the opportunity. Since I was only two years into my corporate work experience, I was simultaneously thrilled and a little nervous.

In those first few months, I compared myself to other sales leaders I respected. Most of them were extroverted, charismatic, well-spoken, and would confidently stand in front of a room of customers to deliver a presentation. I sometimes felt different. I consider myself an ambivert, a balance of extroverted and introverted, but I recharge my energy by spending time alone or with a small group of people I know well. This puts me more on the introverted side of the scale. While I enjoy people and presenting to others, I felt I required more solo preparation and practice than others. As a result, I questioned my ability to lead teams as effectively as others.

Soon after this feeling started to settle in, I received my first feedback from my teams and our first business results. I was very happy to see my teams performing very well against our targets, and more importantly to me, I received positive feedback about how I was leading the team. They specifically shared their appreciation for my openness to discuss their successes and challenges, knowing I would always support them personally and professionally.

From that moment forward, I recognized there are many ways to successfully lead a team and deliberately pursued ways to create psychological safety. I didn't always get it right, but I tried to learn from my failures and continually iterate in every interaction I had with my teams and clients. If I conservatively estimate that I practiced creating an inclusive environment four hours a day for 48 weeks a year, across all 12 years of management, I would have practiced more than 11,000 hours.

I do not believe I will ever claim to be an expert in psychological safety but based on the feedback I've received from my teams and leadership, I know I have created safe spaces more often than not. At this point, I am more likely to recognize when I feel a tension related to wanting to be right about something, so I can share my perspective and proactively invite others. I try to stop myself from immediately sharing my thoughts about a situation, and instead allow others to talk first. I try to recognize differing preferences across my teams. Some prefer to share ideas in a group meeting. Others prefer one-to-one conversations or surveys, sometimes anonymous. I try to give a voice to each person; in a way they prefer. I try to equally embrace compliments and criticism, and I acknowledge when I feel uncomfortable with either type of feedback.

Through all this practice, I have found myself experiencing flow in many moments related to creating psychological safety, and I am still most likely to feel flow during solo planning or reflection. This often happens for me when I am writing or creating a visual that will guide a future conversation, and my environment matters. My current environment is a perfect example. As I write these sentences, I am breathing fresh air through open windows, hearing birds chirping, and regularly looking outside into a neighborhood filled with fully grown and lush green trees, allowing the words to flow from my fingers to the keyboard and onto my screen. I can write many paragraphs not fully recognizing what I am writing because I am in flow. The same is true for the moments when I planned activities for my teams to share their ideas openly with me, sometimes through a guided exercise at an offsite and sometimes through a survey. I would begin the process with an idea and then allow myself the freedom to create, hoping to inspire a meaningful discussion.

Flow can arrive for each of us at different times, and we are more likely to experience it after we have developed a habit of pursuing the skill. The ultra runner can enter flow during her long race because she has created the conditions to allow her mind and body to simply experience the journey. Each of us can find our own opportunity for flow related to psychological safety. But just as Csikszentmihalyi shared, this is not something to force. Flow will happen when the time is right. We just have to allow ourselves the time and space to continually practice, along with the grace for us to know we will sometimes fail and learn along the journey. Through this, we can begin to ensure psychological safety for ourselves, our teams, and organizations. And hopefully over time, we will experience the joy of flow during some of these moments.

What were you doing when you last lost track of time as you pursued a goal?

What from that experience can you integrate into your journey toward psychological safety?

CONCLUSION

My journey to discover psychological safety started when I was a little kid. I recognized early that I wanted to do good things for the world while pursuing a successful career where I could make a lot of money. As I worked through school and considered job options, I often struggled to rectify what I felt were contradictory goals. It wasn't until I found Google that I felt I could enact doing good for the world while making money.

For me, that balance came from embracing psychological safety, and that safety is not limited to those who work at Google. Every one of us has the ability to create feelings of psychological safety where we work, on the teams where we play, and within our families. While many of the stories in this book relate to the business world, we have also seen how psychological safety applies across medicine, nonprofits, athletics, creative endeavors, nature, aviation, personal experiences, and the military.

Our desire for safety is not a passing craze, nor is it likely to subside in the near future.

Our human need for safety started more than 100,000 years ago, originating as our need to avoid getting eaten by a leopard while we tried to find food for ourselves and our family. Today, those of us reading this book are less likely to experience that same physical danger, but we still strive for emotional safety.

When we feel safe, we are able to creatively approach the challenges we face and consider improved alternate approaches to our work. We can celebrate the successes of others, letting go of our ego and openly learning from those who perform better than us. We can also empathetically coach others to become better, with the intent of helping others improve over time.

Effectively implementing psychological safety requires us to find a balance between overt criticism and complacent compliments. This can show up as a criticism that acknowledges a situational challenge, supports the individual to identify ways to improve, and then helps them practice in a safe environment. When we compliment, we can explore ways to share a successful approach with others, to help the broader team and organization learn and improve.

To achieve this, we can start with ourselves. What fears do you face? What motivates you to pursue psychological safety? How can you maintain a growth mindset? In what environment do you work best, and how can you create that environment? How much mental energy can you dedicate to pursuing psychological safety? What holds you back from sharing more, even when you have ideas to improve?

Once we begin to overcome these fears and understand the journey ahead of us, we can create the conditions for ongoing open dialogue with our working teams. Open communication supports each stage of the team engagement, from relationship building through goal achievement. What stories can you share to begin to create connections? How can you create goals aligned to purpose? What discussions can help you align on team decision-making? How can you align the team to take action on the most important goals? How can you create ongoing discussions through feedback, coaching, and modeling?

For most of us in non-executive roles, the final stage is the most difficult to change, but we can still influence our organization's culture. And the effort is worthwhile! Imagine you show up at work tomorrow and everyone, employees and company leadership, has embraced psychological safety.

You and others share ideas openly and with care.

You express your concerns in a way that inspires improvement while providing credit to others for their previous efforts.

You let go of any feelings of ego and the desire to be correct, actively listening to others' ideas and adjusting your approach when appropriate, all in support of achieving mutually beneficial goals.

You and your team have a shared understanding of why you are working toward your goal, not just what you need to achieve.

When you struggle, you ask for help.

When you succeed, you share what worked well, in support of others' efforts to achieve similar goals.

You acknowledge you are on a journey toward creating a working environment that supports your needs and those of others.

You are comfortable acknowledging your biases as you remain curious and open to learn about others.

You breathe a little calmer and your shoulders drop slightly, as the stress you once felt to be perfect begins to subside.

You feel more heard and accepted at work, bringing a smile to your lips a bit more often.

You are more successful because you are constantly learning and improving—failure will happen, and you can learn from it.

Your team achieves more of its goals because you proactively identify, discuss and pursue solutions to upcoming challenges.

Your company is recognized as a great place to work and consistently outperforms its competitors.

You practice creating psychological safety in every interaction.

Psychological safety has permeated your organization.

You will soon close this book or shut down your e-reader with an understanding of the value of psychological safety and tools to consider using. In the next week, I encourage you to select a tool from this book to practice with your team. After you practice for a week, invite a conversation about the tool, share feedback about the experience, listen, and adjust the tool as needed.

Invite: In what ways did the tool help us to communicate more openly, without fear of repercussions? What can we adjust in the tool to further improve our communication?

Share: Allow each team member to share their feedback in the way that feels best for them. Consider email, one-to-one meetings and group meetings.

Listen: Capture key feedback themes and determine appropriate next steps to continue the journey toward psychological safety.

When you and your team begin to feel comfortable with that tool, start practicing with the next.

I wish you, your team, and your organization a fruitful journey, filled with collaborative and challenging discussions that bring joy to the people and success for the business. Happy and successful journeys ahead!

AFTERWORD:
PSYCHOLOGICAL SAFETY WHEN IT'S NEEDED MOST

A registered nurse in an emergency department was caring for a pediatric patient. Lab results indicated the patient could safely return home, but she noticed something different. She recommended the patient be admitted to the hospital, and the physician assistant agreed. The young patient was transferred to the pediatric intensive care unit, where they were treated for a rare and serious condition called multisystem inflammatory syndrome[199]. While most children can recover after receiving medical care, some can die from this condition[200]. She could have saved the child's life by speaking up.

An emergency room nurse recognized a medication was wrongfully ordered for her patient, so she refused to administer it. She helped to protect her patient from harm by speaking up when she knew something was wrong[201].

A hospital nursing assistant recognized a patient was unwell. Instead of remaining silent and trusting the doctors around her to provide all needed care, she persistently spoke up in support of the patient. As a result, the patient promptly received additional care that prevented the condition from worsening[202].

An environmental services associate noticed a patient's labored breathing. The patient's condition appeared to be declining, so she quickly alerted a registered nurse. The nurse was able to take immediate action to avoid the patient reaching a critical situation[203].

These healthcare workers were empowered to provide better patient care because they felt psychologically safe. As a result, the pediatric patient was treated for multisystem inflammatory syndrome. The emergency room patient received the correct medication. The other nurses saved a patient from an otherwise worsening condition and prevented a potentially life-threatening situation.

Each of these individuals are recipients of the Michigan Health & Hospital (MHA) Keystone Center Speak-up! Award. Initiated in March 2016, this quarterly award is intended to recognize individuals and teams who speak-up to prevent potential harm to patients or staff. Through this award, the MHA Keystone Center is helping to ensure people share their concerns and communicate openly, with the hope of eliminating preventable harm caused by miscommunication or non-communication[204].

Adam Novak, Director Safety & Quality at the MHA Keystone Center and creator of the MHA Keystone Center Speak-up! Award compares the award to Toyota's famous jidoka, in which operators are equipped to stop car production any time they perceive something suspicious or troubling[205]. This empowers workers to speak up quickly to stop the production of defective items, so they can fix the problem, reduce waste and increase productivity.

The MHA Keystone Center Speak-up! Award also leads to many benefits. When an employee at an acute care hospital in Michigan shares a concern, the patient receives better care, the physicians and nurses achieve better outcomes, and the hospital can maintain a good reputation. According to Novak, more than half of all Michigan acute care hospitals have voluntarily adopted the MHA Keystone Center Speak-up! Award, with more than 1,200 nominations since its inception. While most of these nominations are to recognize employees who were able to change patient care by voicing their concerns, they also celebrate the moments when employees inadvertently expressed a false alarm.

Novak and others interested in improving patient outcomes would rather someone speak up and be wrong, than to remain silent. Speaking up allows the hospital to pause and reconsider their approach.

Psychological safety was a key consideration when Novak developed the MHA Keystone Center Speak-up! Award, and it is also a direct outcome of the award. The MHA Keystone Center has built a reward system that reinforces that each employee can speak up without fear of repercussions. In other words, they reward psychological safety. And they've done this in an industry that is well-known for struggling to create this safety.

The medical profession is hierarchical, with many nurses feeling they have less authority than doctors when dealing with patients. This can lead to nurses not speaking up during crucial situations, even surgery. Although wrong-site surgeries are rare[206], as many as 2,700 wrong-site procedures occur in the USA every year[207]. This means a surgeon operated on the wrong side of the body, on the wrong appendage, conducted the wrong procedure, or operated on the wrong patient an estimated 40 times a week!

Founded in 1951, The Joint Commission is a nonprofit organization that accredits more than 23,000 healthcare organizations across 70 countries, with the goal of improving patient care and safety. Like the

MHA Keystone Center, The Joint Commission also recognizes the need for open communication to support better patient outcomes. So, they require a discussion as part of The Universal Protocol, a three-step approach to reduce wrong-site surgeries. The final step before starting a surgery is the time-out. During this time-out, everyone on the surgical team must confirm the patient identity, surgical site and procedure to be done. The procedure should not start until all questions and concerns are resolved, allowing everyone in the surgical room to share their opinions, independent of status or role.

The MHA Keystone Center Speak-up! Award and The Universal Protocol time-out provide ways to improve communication. The MHA Keystone Center award celebrates employees who speak up in a moment of need. The time-out specifies when a surgical team will pause and confirm they are pursuing the right surgery. Both reinforce open discussion, feedback, and questioning in support of better patient outcomes. Both create systems that allow for improved psychological safety.

These are two examples of how speaking up can provide a positive impact on individuals and teams, creating better results for workers and those they serve.

ACKNOWLEDGMENTS

Thank you, Colleen, my wife and LOMLs. Your partnership made this book possible. You kept the mini humans entertained as I wrote, brainstormed book content, and helped me think about how to best share this book with the world. Your unwavering support kept me going when I struggled to find the words to put on the page. I love you.

Thank you, Sierra and Jackson. You don't know it yet, but you helped me write this book too. I spent half of my days with you during the book-writing process, and you helped to shift my brain to the more important things in life, like family. You make my life complete and I'm so happy to be around to watch you continue to grow and learn. I love you.

Thank you, Mams and Paps. Whenever anyone would ask about my approach to management, I always shared that I learned all I needed from you. Observing you coach my soccer teams and interact with others throughout my life, you unintentionally and naturally modeled the traits of a great manager. I was very lucky to grow up with parents who communicated openly, directly, and with love. And I'm very lucky to still learn from you every day. I love you.

Thank you, Sis. You are one of the few people in my life who I have always looked up to and tried to emulate. You taught me to love myself for who I am and to ignore the pull to follow the crowd. For as long as I can remember, you have challenged gender norms and fought for equality, celebrating the beauty of diversity. I still remember a conversation from when I was younger, when I said, "pink is for girls." You corrected me and explained pink is for anyone who likes it. You have always helped me and others challenge our assumptions. I love you.

Thank you, Brendon Kraham, Jeff Montgomery, and Shannon Wasiolek. Each of you modeled and created the conditions for psychological safety on your teams. You care deeply about your team members, helping them achieve their personal and professional goals, even when those goals differ from yours. You do this while driving great business outcomes. You are models of great leadership, and anyone would be lucky to work with you.

Thank you, Jenny Wood, Laura Mae Martin, and Mike Figiuolo. Each of you helped me think through my approach to this book. You inspire me with how you manage your careers and through writing your own books. You follow the path that works best for you and I can feel your passion when we talk.

Thank you, Monica Baker and Joni Sensel. I feel very fortunate our paths crossed during this project. Your expertise helped me transform this manuscript into something I am proud to share with the world.

Thank you, Antonio McFadden, Chris Clark, Kate Hanisian, Merri McCann, and Randy Frankel. Each of you contributed ideas or reviewed text that helped me develop a more inclusive book. You guided me toward more appropriate wording and frameworks to enhance interpersonal understanding and help bring people together.

Thank you, Adam Novak, for working with me to ensure the correct language related to the MHA Keystone Center Speak-up! Award. I greatly appreciate your partnership and hope others can learn from what you have done in Michigan.

Finally, but definitely not least, thank you to all the Googlers I worked with from 2007 through 2022. None of this would be possible without each of you on my teams and beyond. I will always cherish the memory of working with you, and I hope our paths cross again.

ABOUT THE AUTHOR

David Moerlein has created psychologically safe spaces at work for more than a decade. During his 15 years at Google, he managed hundreds of people across ten global offices within sales, customer service, and enablement. His teams worked with thousands of Google Ads customers, launched Google's first seller skills training to the SMB sales organization, won a Brandon Hall Award for a project he co-led in support of Google's managers, and consistently exceeded enablement benchmarks for global training. David was awarded the Lombardi Award for Coaching Excellence, Top SMB Manager Award, Top 10 Manager Award, and was nominated by his teams for multiple other awards.

Prior to Google, David received his MBA with Distinction from the University of Michigan, a full academic scholarship for his MS in Biology from the University of Cincinnati, and his BA in Ecology from the University of Colorado Boulder. He was awarded memberships into Phi Beta Kappa and Golden Key International Honour Society.

David lives in Cincinnati, Ohio, with his wife Colleen, daughter Sierra, son Jackson, and dog Cooper. When not enjoying time with his family or writing, he is usually training for triathlons or planning his next outdoor adventure.

NOTES

[1] Wolverton, B.C., Anne Johnson, and Keith Bounds. "Interior Landscape Plants for Indoor Air Pollution Abatement." *National Aeronautics and Space Administration*, (1989). Accessed November 1, 2023.

[2] "Alphabet Inc Class C GOOG." Morningstar. June 12, 2023.

[3] Alphabet Inc. *Form 10-K 2022*. Mountain View, CA: Alphabet Inc, 2022.

[4] "Helpful Products. Built with You in Mind." About Google. Accessed June 12, 2023. https://about.google/intl/en_us/products/#all-products.

[5] Silverstein, Ken. "Google Has Invested $3.5 Billion In Renewable Energy Projects Worldwide." Environment + Energy LEADER. May 26, 2022. https://www.environmentalleader.com/2022/05/google-has-invested-3-5-billion-in-renewable-energy-projects-worldwide/.

[6] Schein, Edgar H., and Warren G. Bennis. 1965. *Personal and Organizational Change Through Group Methods: The Laboratory Approach*. Wiley.

[7] "Psychological Safety." Amy C. Edmondson. Accessed June 12, 2023. https://amycedmondson.com/psychological-safety/#triage.

[8] "Guide: Understand Team Effectiveness." Re: Work. Google Inc, Accessed June 12, 2023. https://rework.withgoogle.com/print/guides/5721312655835136/.

[9] Edmondson, Amy C. 2018. *The Fearless Organization: Creating Psychological Safety in the Workplace for Learning, Innovation, and Growth*, 159. Wiley.

[10] Radecki, Dan, Leonie Hull, Jennifer McCusker, and Christopher Ancona. 2018. *Psychological Safety: The Key to Happy, High-performing People and Teams*. The Academy of Brain-based Leadership.

[11] Clark, Timothy R. 2020. *The 4 Stages of Psychological Safety: Defining the Path to Inclusion and Innovation*. Berrett-Koehler Publishers.

[12] Helbig, Karolin, and Minette Norman. 2023. *The Psychological Safety Playbook: Lead More Powerfully by Being More Human*. Page Two Press.

[13] "2023 F-150 XLT." Ford. Accessed April 27, 2023. https://www.ford.com/trucks/f150/models/f150-xlt/.

[14] Handwerk, Brian. "An Evolutionary Timeline of Homo Sapiens." Smithsonian Magazine. February 2, 2021. https://www.smithsonianmag.com/science-nature/essential-timeline-understanding-evolution-homo-sapiens-180976807/.

[15] Dunn, Rob. "The Top Ten Deadliest Animals of Our Evolutionary Past." Smithsonian Magazine. June 20, 2011. https://www.smithsonianmag.com/science-nature/the-top-ten-deadliest-animals-of-our-evolutionary-past-18257965/.

[16] Takac, Marcel, James Collett, Kristopher J. Blom, Russell Conduit, Imogen Rehm, and Alexander De Foe. "Public Speaking Anxiety Decreases within Repeated Virtual Reality Training Sessions." *PLoS One*, (2019). Accessed August 15, 2023. https://doi.org/10.1371/journal.pone.0216288.

[17] Eisenberger, Naomi I. "The Neural Bases of Social Pain: Evidence for Shared Representations with Physical Pain." *Psychosom Med*, (2012). Accessed October 30, 2023. https://doi.org/10.1097/PSY.0b013e3182464dd1.

[18] "Guide: Understand Team Effectiveness." Re:Work. Google Inc, Accessed June 12, 2023. https://rework.withgoogle.com/print/guides/5721312655835136/.

[19] Edmondson, *The Fearless Organization,* xvi.

[20] Edmondson, *The Fearless Organization*, 53, 60, 63.

[21] Hotten, Russell. "Volkswagen: The Scandal Explained." BBC. December 10, 2015. https://www.bbc.com/news/business-34324772.

22 "Volkswagen Says Diesel Scandal Has Cost It 31.3 Billion Euros." Reuters. March 17, 2020. https://www.reuters.com/article/us-volkswagen-results-diesel/volkswagen-says-diesel-scandal-has-cost-it-31-3-billion-euros-idUSKBN2141JB.

23 Kelly, Jack. "Wells Fargo Forced to Pay $3 Billion For The Bank's Fake Account Scandal." *Forbes*. February 24, 2020. https://www.forbes.com/sites/jackkelly/2020/02/24/wells-fargo-forced-to-pay-3-billion-for-the-banks-fake-account-scandal/?sh=1c92023742d2.

24 Huy, Quy, and Timo Vuori. "Who Killed Nokia? Nokia Did." Insead Knowledge. September 22, 2015. https://knowledge.insead.edu/strategy/who-killed-nokia-nokia-did.

25 Monet, Torin. "Why Psychological Safety at Work Matters to Business." Accenture. October 28, 2021. https://www.accenture.com/us-en/blogs/business-functions-blog/work-psychological-safety.

26 Catmull, Ed, and Amy Wallace. 2014. *Creativity, Inc.: Overcoming the Unseen Forces That Stand in the Way of True Inspiration*. Random House.

27 Edmondson, *The Fearless Organization*, 104.

28 Whitten, Sarah. "Bob Iger Says Pixar Was 'Probably the Best' Acquisition He Made during His Tenure with Disney." CNBC. December 21, 2021. https://www.cnbc.com/2021/12/21/disneys-bob-iger-says-pixar-was-probably-the-best-acquisition-as-ceo.html.

29 Warnick, Jennifer. "Inside the Tryer Center, the Starbucks Lab where Anything Is Possible." Starbucks Stories & News. June 11, 2019. https://stories.starbucks.com/stories/2019/inside-the-tryer-center-the-starbucks-lab-where-anything-is-possible/.

30 Rainey, Clint. "What Happened to Starbucks? How a Progressive Company Lost Its Way." Fast Company. March 17, 2022. https://www.fastcompany.com/90732166/what-happened-to-starbucks-how-a-progressive-company-lost-its-way.

31 "Starbucks Corp SBUX." Morningstar. Accessed July 12, 2023. https://www.morningstar.com/stocks/xnas/sbux/quote.

32 "JDE Peet's N.V." Yahoo! Finance. Accessed July 12, 2023. https://finance.yahoo.com/quote/JDEP.AS/.

33 Fantozzi, Joanna. "Inspire Brands Completes Purchase of Dunkin' Brands Group for $11.3 Billion." Nation's Restaurant News. December 15, 2020.

https://www.nrn.com/quick-service/inspire-brands-completes-purchase-dunkin-brands-group-113-billion.

[34] "Dutch Bros Inc Class A BROS" Morningstar. Accessed July 12, 2023.

[35] "Starbucks Revenue 2010-2023 | SBUX." Macrotrends. Accessed July 12, 2023.
https://www.macrotrends.net/stocks/charts/SBUX/starbucks/revenue.

[36] Brutsche, Kimberly, and Tiarra McDaniel. "How Psychological Safety Creates Cohesion: A Leader's Guide." U.S. Army. April 27, 2021.
https://www.army.mil/article/245626/how_psychological_safety_creates_co hesion_a_leaders_guide#:~:text=To%20create%20the%20psychological%20 safety,rejection%2C%20punishment%2C%20or%20ostracization.

[37] "Moray." Britannica. April 11, 2023.
https://www.britannica.com/animal/moray-eel.

[38] "Pacific Cleaner Shrimp." Aquarium of the Pacific. Accessed June 14, 2023.
https://www.aquariumofpacific.org/onlinelearningcenter/species/pacific_cle aner_shrimp.

[39] Wikipedia. 2023. "Cleaner Shrimp." Wikimedia Foundation. Last modified July 25, 2023. https://en.wikipedia.org/wiki/Cleaner_shrimp.

[40] Lencioni, Patrick M. 2011. *The Five Dysfunctions of a Team: A Leadership Fable.* Jossey-Bass.

[41] Maister, David H., Charles H. Green, and Robert M. Galford. 2001. *The Trusted Advisor: 20th Anniversary Edition.* Free Press.

[42] Offermann, Lynn, and Lisa Rosh. "Building Trust Through Skillful Self-Disclosure." *Harvard Business Review.* June 13, 2012.
https://hbr.org/2012/06/instantaneous-intimacy-skillfu.

[43] Dirks, Kurt T., and Donald L. Ferrin. "Trust in Leadership: Meta-analytic Findings and Implications for Research and Practice." *Journal of Applied Psychology*, (2002). Accessed October 30, 2023. https://doi.org/10.1037/0021-9010.87.4.611.

[44] Zak, Paul J. "The Neuroscience of Trust." *Harvard Business Review.* February 1, 2017. https://hbr.org/2017/01/the-neuroscience-of-trust.

[45] Wood, Nathanael, Sam Straw, Mattia Scalabrin, Lee D. Roberts, Klaus K. Witte, and Thomas S. Bowen. "Skeletal Muscle Atrophy in Heart Failure with Diabetes: From Molecular Mechanisms to Clinical Evidence." *ESC Heart Fail*, (2021). Accessed October 30, 2023. https://doi.org/10.1002/ehf2.13121.

[46] "What Is Cognitive Behavioral Therapy?" American Psychological Association. January 1, 2017. https://www.apa.org/ptsd-guideline/patients-and-families/cognitive-behavioral.

[47] Schat, Aaron, and Michael R. Frone. "Exposure to Psychological Aggression at Work and Job Performance: The Mediating Role of Job Attitudes and Personal Health." *Work Stress*, (2011). Accessed October 30, 2023. https://doi.org/10.1080/02678373.2011.563133.

[48] "Women in the Workplace 2022." McKinsey & Company. October 18, 2022. https://www.mckinsey.com/featured-insights/diversity-and-inclusion/women-in-the-workplace.

[49] "Diversity Wins: How Inclusion Matters." McKinsey & Company. May 19, 2020. https://www.mckinsey.com/featured-insights/diversity-and-inclusion/diversity-wins-how-inclusion-matters.

[50] Wikipedia. 2023. "Tenerife Airport Disaster." Wikimedia Foundation. Last modified October 27, 2023. https://en.wikipedia.org/wiki/Tenerife_airport_disaster.

[51] McCreary, John, Michael Pollard, Kenneth Stevenson, and Marc B. Wilson. "Human Factors: Tenerife Revisited." *Journal of Air Transportation World Wide*, (1998). Accessed October 30, 2023.

[52] Edmondson, *The Fearless Organization*, 79.

[53] Leary, Mark R. "Emotional Responses to Interpersonal Rejection." *Dialogues in Clinical Neuroscience*, (2015). Accessed October 31, 2023. https://doi.org/10.31887/DCNS.2015.17.4/mleary.

[54] Nicholls, Michael E. R., Owen Churches, and Tobias Loetscher. "Perception of an Ambiguous Figure Is Affected by Own-age Social Biases." *Scientific Reports*, (2018). Accessed October 31, 2023. https://doi.org/10.1038/s41598-018-31129-7.

[55] Woods, Rose A. "Spotlight on Statistics: Sports and Exercise." U.S. Bureau of Labor Statistics. May 1, 2017. https://www.bls.gov/spotlight/2017/sports-and-exercise/home.htm.

[56] "5 Surprising Benefits of Walking." Harvard Health Publishing: Harvard Medical School. August 25, 2022. https://www.health.harvard.edu/staying-healthy/5-surprising-benefits-of-walking.

[57] DeVore, Jessica, Dan Gouthro, and Chris Mullen. "The Heard and the Heard-Nots." *Workforce Institute*. Accessed November 1, 2023.

58 National Academies of Sciences, Engineering, and Medicine. 2018. How People Learn II: Learners, Contexts, and Cultures. Washington, DC: The National Academies Press.

59 Pink, Daniel H. 2011. *Drive: The Surprising Truth About What Motivates Us.* Riverhead Books.

60 Deci, Edward L. "Effects of Externally Mediated Rewards on Intrinsic Motivation." *Journal of Personality and Social Psychology*, (1971). Accessed November 1, 2023. https://doi.org/10.1037/h0030644.

61 Cho, Yoon J., and James L. Perry. "Intrinsic Motivation and Employee Attitudes Role of Managerial Trustworthiness, Goal Directedness, and Extrinsic Reward Expectancy." *Review of Public Personnel Administration*, (2012). Accessed November 1, 2023. https://doi.org/10.1177/0734371X11421495.

62 Schwantes, Marcel. "Studies Show 91 Percent of Us Won't Achieve Our New Year's Resolutions. How to Be the 9 Percent That Do." *Inc.*, January 8, 2022. https://www.inc.com/marcel-schwantes/studies-show-91-percent-of-us-wont-achieve-our-new-years-resolutions-how-to-be-9-percent-that-do.html#:~:text=Studies%20I've%20read%20over,quit%20your%20New%20Year's%20goals.

63 Zhang, Leigang, and Yuzhu Zhang. "The Mediating Effect of Self-Regulation on the Association Between Growth Mindset About Work and Living a Calling Among Primary and Secondary School Teachers." *Psychol Res Behav Manag.*, (2021). Accessed November 1, 2023. https://doi.org/10.2147/PRBM.S330961.

64 Dweck, Carol S. 2006. *Mindset: The New Psychology of Success.* Random House.

65 Kahneman, Daniel. 2011. *Thinking, Fast and Slow.* Farrar, Straus and Giroux.

66 "CDC Museum COVID-19 Timeline." Centers for Disease Control and Prevention. March 15, 2023. https://www.cdc.gov/museum/timeline/covid19.html#:~:text=January%2010%2C%202020,Coronavirus%20(2019%2DnCoV).

67 "Past Flu Pandemics." Centers for Disease Control and Prevention. August 10, 2018. https://www.cdc.gov/flu/pandemic-resources/basics/past-pandemics.html.

68 Wikipedia. 2023. "List of Epidemics and Pandemics." Wikimedia Foundation. Last modified November 1, 2023. https://en.wikipedia.org/wiki/List_of_epidemics_and_pandemics.

[69] "Mental Health and COVID-19: Early Evidence of the Pandemic's Impact." *World Health Organization*, (2022). Accessed November 1, 2023.

[70] "Looking After Our Mental Health." World Health Organization. Accessed June 15, 2023. https://www.who.int/campaigns/connecting-the-world-to-combat-coronavirus/healthyathome/healthyathome---mental-health.

[71] Parkhurst, Emma. "How Hobbies Improve Mental Health." Utah State University. October 25, 2021. https://extension.usu.edu/mentalhealth/articles/how-hobbies-improve-mental-health.

[72] "53% Who Took on a Pandemic Hobby Went Into Credit Card Debt as a Result." PR Newswire. April 6, 2021. https://www.prnewswire.com/news-releases/53-who-took-on-a-pandemic-hobby-went-into-credit-card-debt-as-a-result-301263449.html.

[73] Haroun, Azmi. "The Pandemic Spurred a Legion of Young Shredders.16 Million People Have Taken up the Guitar, Fender Says." Insider. October 7, 2021. https://www.businessinsider.com/16-million-people-have-taken-up-guitar-over-pandemic-fender-2021-10.

[74] Wikipedia. 2023. "Sister Rosetta Tharpe." Wikimedia Foundation. Last modified November 9, 2023. https://en.wikipedia.org/wiki/Sister_Rosetta_Tharpe.

[75] Big thanks to … "Brady Rennell." Director of Development, The University of Texas at Austin. Accessed November 8, 2023. https://www.linkedin.com/in/bradyrennell/.

[76] Latane, Bibb, and John M. Darley. "Group Inhibition of Bystander Intervention in Emergencies." *Journal of Personality and Social Psychology*, (1968). Accessed November 1, 2023. https://doi.org/10.1037/h0026570.

[77] Darley, John M., and Bibb Latane. "Bystander Intervention in Emergencies: Diffusion of Responsibility." *Journal of Personality and Social Psychology*, (1968). Accessed November 1, 2023. https://doi.org/10.1037/h0025589.

[78] Hatfield, Elaine, John T. Cacioppo, and Richard L. Rapson. "Primitive Emotional Contagion." *Emotion and Social Behavior*, (1992). Accessed November 1, 2023. https://doi.org/10.1017/CBO9781139174138.

[79] Simner, Marvin L. "Newborn's Response to the Cry of Another Infant." *Developmental Psychology*, (1971). Accessed November 1, 2023. https://doi.org/10.1037/h0031066.

80 Van Baaren, Rick B., Rob W. Holland, Kerry Kawakami, and Ad Van Knippenberg. "Mimicry and Prosocial Behavior." *Psychological Science*, (2004). Accessed November 1, 2023. https://doi.org/10.1111/j.0963-7214.2004.01501012.x.

81 Clance, Pauline R., and Suzanne A. Imes. "The Imposter Phenomenon in High Achieving Women: Dynamics and Therapeutic Intervention." *Psychotherapy: Theory, Research & Practice*, (1978). Accessed November 1, 2023. https://doi.org/10.1037/h0086006.

82 Bravata, Dena M., Sharon A. Watts, Autumn L. Keefer, Divya K. Madhusudhan, Katie T. Taylor, Dani M. Clark, Ross S. Nelson, Kevin O. Cokley, and Heather K. Hagg. "Prevalence, Predictors, and Treatment of Impostor Syndrome: A Systematic Review." *Journal of General Internal Medicine*, (2020). Accessed November 1, 2023. https://doi.org/10.1007/s11606-019-05364-1.

83 Voiland, Adam. "Saving a Forest of One." NASA: Earth Observatory. Accessed November 1, 2023. https://earthobservatory.nasa.gov/images/151022/saving-a-forest-of-one#:~:text=Pando%27s%20trees%20and%20root%20system,land%20organisms%20on%20the%20planet.

84 Guan, Li, and Qi Wang. "Does Sharing Memories Make Us Feel Closer? The Roles of Memory Type and Culture." *Journal of Cross-Cultural Psychology*, (2022). Accessed November 1, 2023. https://doi.org/10.1177/00220221211072809.

85 Edmondson, *The Fearless Organization,* 11.

86 Sutton, Bob. "Why Big Teams Suck: Seven (Plus or Minus Two) Is the Magical Number Once Again." Bob Sutton: Work Matters. March 3, 2014. https://bobsutton.typepad.com/my_weblog/2014/03/why-big-teams-suck-seven-plus-or-minus-two-is-the-magical-number-once-again.html.

87 Miller, George A. "The Magical Number Seven, plus or minus Two: Some Limits on Our Capacity for Processing Information." *Psychological Review*, (1956). Accessed November 1, 2023. https://doi.org/10.1037/h0043158.

88 "Bluey: Awards." IMDb. Accessed June 15, 2023. https://www.imdb.com/title/tt7678620/awards/.

89 "Bluey: The Australian Cartoon That's Going Global." BBC. August 1, 2019. https://www.bbc.com/news/av/world-australia-49175684.

[90] Quinn, Karl. "Sixty Countries, 110 Licences, 1000 Products: How Bluey Conquered the World." The Sydney Morning Herald. June 14, 2022. https://www.smh.com.au/culture/tv-and-radio/how-bluey-went-from-a-kids-tv-show-to-a-global-merchandising-machine-20220610-p5asxg.html.

[91] Tait, Amelia. "The Internet Is Breeding Hordes of Adult Bluey Fans." Wired. January 23, 2023. https://www.wired.com/story/bluey-internet-fandom/.

[92] Brumberg, Robby. "Lessons on Life, Writing and Storytelling from the Creator of 'Bluey'." Ragan. April 7, 2021. https://www.ragan.com/lessons-on-life-writing-and-storytelling-from-the-creator-of-bluey/.

[93] Castro, Dotan R., Frederik Anseel, Avraham N. Kluger, Karina J. Lloyd, and Yaara Turjeman-Levi. "Mere Listening Effect on Creativity and the Mediating Role of Psychological Safety." Psychology of Aesthetics, (2018). Accessed November 1, 2023. https://doi.org/10.1037/aca0000177.

[94] Fenniman, Andrew. "Understanding Each Other at Work: An Examination of the Effects of Perceived Empathetic Listening on Psychological Safety in the Supervisor-Subordinate Relationship." Dissertation Abstracts International Section A: Humanities and Social Sciences, (2010). Accessed November 1, 2023.

[95] Avraham, Kluger N., and Guy Itzchakov. "The Power of Listening at Work." Annual Review of Organizational Psychology and Organizational Behavior, (2022). Accessed November 1, 2023. https://doi.org/10.1146/annurev-orgpsych-012420-091013.

[96] "Brendon Kraham." Vice President, Global Search Ads and Commerce, Business & Product Strategy, Google. Accessed November 8, 2023. https://www.linkedin.com/in/brendonkraham/.

[97] "Looking for StrengthsFinder? You're in the Right Place." Gallup. Accessed June 15, 2023. https://www.gallup.com/cliftonstrengths/en/254033/strengthsfinder.aspx.

[98] "Insights Discovery." Insights. Accessed June 15, 2023. https://www.insights.com/us/products/insights-discovery/.

[99] "True Colors Temperament & Personality Typing Programs." True Colors: Valuing Differences - Creating Unity. Accessed June 15, 2023. https://www.truecolorsintl.com/about.

[100] Sandberg, Sheryl. 2013. Lean In: Women, Work, and the Will to Lead. Knopf.

[101] Alexander, Michelle. 2020. The New Jim Crow: Mass Incarceration in the Age of Colorblindness. The New Press.

[102] Boyd, Graham. "The Drug War Is the New Jim Crow." ACLU. July 31, 2001. https://www.aclu.org/documents/drug-war-new-jim-crow.

[103] Noah, Trevor. 2016. *Born a Crime: Stories from a South African Childhood*. One World.

[104] Duhigg, Charles. 2012. *The Power of Habit: Why We Do What We Do in Life and Business*. Random House.

[105] DuVernay, Ava, director. *13th: From Slave To Criminal With One Amendment*. Netflix, 2016.

[106] Moudatsou, Maria, Areti Stavropoulou, Anastas Philalithis, and Sofia Koukouli. "The Role of Empathy in Health and Social Care Professionals." *Healthcare*, (2020). Accessed November 1, 2023. https://doi.org/10.3390/healthcare8010026.

[107] "How to Open a Banana? They're Fun to Peel!" Chiquita. November 30, 2020. https://www.chiquita.com/blog/how-to-open-a-banana-theyre-fun-to-peel/.

[108] Wikipedia. 2023. "Blind Men and an Elephant." Wikimedia Foundation. Last modified October 26, 2023. https://en.wikipedia.org/wiki/Blind_men_and_an_elephant#:~:text=The%20moral%20of%20the%20parable,it%20has%20been%20widely%20diffused.

[109] "Population Density (People per Sq. Km of Land Area) - Haiti, United States, France, Jamaica." The World Bank. Accessed July 3, 2023. https://data.worldbank.org/indicator/EN.POP.DNST?end=2020&locations=HT-US-FR-JM&start=1961.

[110] "The World Bank in Haiti. The World Bank." The World Bank. March 31, 2023. https://www.worldbank.org/en/country/haiti/overview.

[111] Arnaouti, Matthew K. C., Gabrielle Cahill, Michael D. Baird, Laelle Mangurat, Rachel Harris, Louidort P. P. Edme, Michelle N. Joseph, Tamara Worlton, and Sylvio Augustin Jr. "Medical Disaster Response: A Critical Analysis of the 2010 Haiti Earthquake." *Frontiers in Public Health*, (2022). Accessed November 1, 2023. https://doi.org/10.3389/fpubh.2022.995595.

[112] "Haiti In Ruins: A Look Back At The 2010 Earthquake." NPR. January 12, 2020. https://www.npr.org/sections/pictureshow/2020/01/12/794939899/haiti-in-ruins-a-look-back-at-the-2010-earthquake.

[113] "Haiti: An Overview of MSF Operations in 2010." Doctors Without Borders. December 20, 2010. The author is in no way affiliated with Doctors

Without Borders/Médecins Sans Frontières (MSF).
https://www.doctorswithoutborders.org/latest/haiti-overview-msf-operations-2010. All views expressed herein are exclusively those of the author.

114 "Human Wellbeing: Taking Action." *Doctors Without Borders,*. Accessed July 3, 2023. https://msf.org.au/sites/default/files/attachments/7_-_stage_5_human_wellbeing_-_taking_action.pdf.

115 "Haiti." Centers for Disease Control and Prevention. January 25, 2023. https://www.cdc.gov/cholera/haiti/index.html

116 "Population, Total—Haiti." The World Bank. Accessed July 3, 2023. https://data.worldbank.org/indicator/SP.POP.TOTL?locations=HT.

117 "Our History: Founded to Save Lives and Speak Out, MSF Teams Have Cared for Tens of Millions of People since 1971." Doctors Without Borders. Accessed July 3, 2023. https://www.doctorswithoutborders.org/who-we-are/our-history.

118 "Who We Are: Every Day, Doctors Without Borders Teams Deliver Emergency Medical Aid to People in Crisis, with Humanitarian Projects in More than 70 Countries." Doctors Without Borders. Accessed July 3, 2023. https://www.doctorswithoutborders.org/who-we-are

119 "The Nobel Peace Prize." Doctors Without Borders. Accessed July 3, 2023. https://www.msf-me.org/about-us/history/nobel-peaceprize#:~:text=Dr%20Orbinski%20then%20spoke%20freely,no%20humanitarian%20can%20make%20peace.

120 Caldron, Paul H. " 'Fit' for Service: Contrasting Physician Profiles and Motivations for Short-term Medical Missions and MéDecins Sans FrontièRes." *Journal of Compassionate Health Care*, (2017). Accessed November 1, 2023. https://doi.org/10.1186/s40639-017-0038-y.

121 "How Great Leaders Inspire Action | Simon Sinek." TED. May 4, 2010. Video, https://www.youtube.com/watch?v=qp0HIF3SfI4.

122 "Rohingya Refugee Crisis." Doctors Without Borders. March 15, 2018. https://www.doctorswithoutborders.org/what-we-do/focus/rohingya-refugee-crisis.

123 "How We Work: Discover How We Deliver Medical Humanitarian Assistance." Doctors Without Borders. Accessed July 4, 2023. https://www.msf.org/how-we-work.

124 "The Power of Vulnerability | Brené Brown." TED. January 3, 2011. Video, https://www.youtube.com/watch?v=iCvmsMzlF7o.

125 Platt, Michael, Vera Ludwig, Elizabeth Johnson, and Per Hugander. "Perspective Taking: A Brain Hack That Can Help You Make Better Decisions." Knowledge at Wharton. March 22, 2021. https://knowledge.wharton.upenn.edu/article/perspective-taking-brain-hack-can-help-make-better-decisions/.

126 Suttie, Jill. "Does Venting Your Feelings Actually Help?" Greater Good Magazine: Science-Based Insights for a Meaningful Life. June 21, 2021. https://greatergood.berkeley.edu/article/item/does_venting_your_feelings_a ctually_help.

127 Pace, Karen L. "The Myth of Multitasking: Research Says It Makes Us Less Productive and Increases Mistakes." Michigan State University. March 31, 2017. https://www.canr.msu.edu/news/the_myth_of_multitasking_research_says_ it_makes_us_less_productive_and_incr#:~:text=Ask%20Extension,The%20 myth%20of%20multitasking%3A%20Research%20says%20it%20makes,less %20productive%20and%20increases%20mistakes&text=Many%20people%2 0multitask%20because%20they,on%20our%20time%20and%20attention.

128 "Mike Figliuolo." thoughtLEADERS, LLC, www.thoughtleadersllc.com/team/Mike-Figliuolo.

129 "How to Foster Psychological Safety on Your Teams." Re:Work With Google. Accessed August 21, 2023. https://docs.google.com/document/d/1PsnDMS2emcPLgMLFAQCXZjO7 C4j2hJ7znOq_g2Zkjgk/edit.

130 "Chip Heath: The Thrive Foundation for Youth Professor of Organizational Behavior, Emeritus." Stanford Business. Accessed July 4, 2023. https://www.gsb.stanford.edu/faculty-research/faculty/chip-heath

131 "Dan Heath." Duke Fuqua. Accessed July 4, 2023. https://centers.fuqua.duke.edu/case/team_profiles/dan-heath/.

132 Heath, Chip, and Dan Heath. 2010. *Switch: How to Change Things When Change Is Hard.* Crown Currency.

133 Oliveros, Feli. "U.S. Employees Are Distracted Every 31 Minutes on Average." Value Penguin by Lending Tree. June 23, 2021. https://www.valuepenguin.com/news/employee-distractions-productivity.

[134] Griffey, Harriet. "The Lost Art of Concentration: Being Distracted in a Digital World." *The Guardian*. October 14, 2018. https://www.theguardian.com/lifeandstyle/2018/oct/14/the-lost-art-of-concentration-being-distracted-in-a-digital-world.

[135] Cooper, Bailey. "What Is Important Is Seldom Urgent and What Is Urgent Is Seldom Important. Dwight D. Eisenhower." LinkedIn. March 30, 2016. https://www.linkedin.com/pulse/what-important-seldom-urgent-dwight-d-eisenhower-bailey-cooper/.

[136] Covey, Stephen R., A. Roger Merrill, and Rebecca R. Merrill. 2015. *First Things First*. Franklin Covey.

[137] Acar, Oguz A., Murat Tarakci, and Daan Van Knippenberg. "Creativity and Innovation Under Constraints: A Cross-Disciplinary Integrative Review." *Journal of Management*, (2019). Accessed November 1, 2023. https://doi.org/10.1177/0149206318805832.

[138] "Atul Gawande: About." Atul Gawande. Accessed July 5, 2023. https://atulgawande.com/about/.

[139] Gawande, Atul. 2009. *The Checklist Manifesto: How to Get Things Right*. Metropolitan Books.

[140] Loder, Vanessa. "Why Multi-Tasking Is Worse Than Marijuana For Your IQ." *Forbes*. June 11, 2014. https://www.forbes.com/sites/vanessaloder/2014/06/11/why-multi-tasking-is-worse-than-marijuana-for-your-iq/?sh=4e91e2ab7c11.

[141] Wikipedia. 2023. "Group Development." Wikimedia Foundation. Last modified April 30, 2023. https://en.wikipedia.org/wiki/Group_development.

[142] "Coach Pat Summitt: 1952-2016." UT Sports. Accessed November 3, 2023. https://utsports.com/sports/2017/6/20/coach-pat-summitt-1952-2016.aspx.

[143] "The Story of Pat Summitt's First National Title at Tennessee." SEC Network. February 20, 2023. Video, https://www.facebook.com/watch/?v=1945114392502699.

[144] "The Definite Dozen." Pat Summitt Foundation. Accessed November 3, 2023. https://www.patsummitt.org/coach-summitt/the-definite-dozen.

[145] Smith, Jason. "Fellow Coaches, Former Players Say Pat Summitt Left a Lasting Impact." Commercial Appeal. June 28, 2016. https://www.commercialappeal.com/story/sports/college/southeastern-

conference/2016/06/28/fellow-coaches-former-players-say-pat-summitt-left-a-lasting-impact/90568020/.

[146] Hall, Cora. "What Lady Vols Legend Candace Parker Said About New Documentary, Motherhood and Pat Summitt." Knox News. October 24, 2023. https://www.knoxnews.com/story/sports/college/university-of-tennessee/womens-basketball/2023/10/24/candace-parker-lady-vols-basketball-pat-summitt-documentary-motherhood-espnw-summit/71305562007/.

[147] "The Definite Dozen." Pat Summitt Foundation. Accessed November 3, 2023. https://www.patsummitt.org/coach-summitt/the-definite-dozen.

[148] Zenger, Jack, and Joseph Folkman. "The Ideal Praise-to-Criticism Ratio." Harvard Business Review. March 15, 2013. https://hbr.org/2013/03/the-ideal-praise-to-criticism.

[149] Atkinson, Adelle, Christopher J. Watling, and Paul L. P. Brand. "Feedback and Coaching." *European Journal of Pediatrics*, (2022). Accessed November 3, 2023. https://doi.org/10.1007/s00431-021-04118-8.

[150] Hardavella, Georgia, Ane Aamli-Gaagnat, Neil Saad, Ilona Rousalova, and Katherina B. Sreter. "How to Give and Receive Feedback Effectively." *Breathe (Sheffield, England)*, (2017). Accessed November 3, 2023. https://doi.org/10.1183/20734735.009917.

[151] Pendleton, David, Theo Schofield, and Peter Tate. 1984. *The Consultation: An Approach to Learning and Teaching*. Oxford University Press.

[152] The GROW Model was first published by Sir John Whitmore, co-founder of Performance Consultants, in 1992 in his book Coaching for Performance. A full explanation of The GROW Model can be found in the book's Fifth Edition at Chapters 9-13 (Whitmore and Performance Consultants, 2017). Learn more at https://www.performanceconsultants.com/grow-model

[153] "OUCH! Our Unconscious Controlling Habits — What Is Your Worst Habit as a Manager?" CEQ - Collaborative Equity. June 6, 2021. Video, https://www.youtube.com/watch?v=24-Yj4bn5w0.

[154] "Instructional Moves: Providing Wait-Time for Students to Process and Gain Confidence." Harvard Graduate School of Education. Accessed July 5, 2023. https://instructionalmoves.gse.harvard.edu/providing-wait-time-students-process-and-gain-confidence.

[155] Clark, Timothy R. 2020. *The 4 Stages of Psychological Safety: Defining the Path to Inclusion and Innovation*. Berrett-Koehler Publishers.

156 Alphabet Inc. *Form 10-Q*. Mountain View, CA: Alphabet Inc, 2023.

157 "Bring a Creative Project to Life." Kickstarter. Accessed May 16, 2023. https://www.kickstarter.com/.

158 "About Us." Airbnb News. Accessed July 6, 2023. https://news.airbnb.com/about-us/.

159 "Revenue of the LEGO Group from 2003 to 2022." Statista. Accessed July 6, 2023. https://www.statista.com/statistics/282870/lego-group-revenue/.

160 Whitten, Sarah. "Lego Revenue Jumped 27% in 2021, as Kids and Adults Continue to Build." CNBC. March 8, 2022. https://www.cnbc.com/2022/03/08/lego-revenue-jumped-27percent-in-2021-as-kids-and-adults-continue-to-build.html.

161 "It's Your Time to Shine!" LEGO Ideas. Accessed November 4, 2023. https://ideas.lego.com/projects/create.

162 Wikipedia. 2023. "Lego Ideas." Wikimedia Foundation. Last modified October 13, 2023. https://en.wikipedia.org/wiki/Lego_Ideas.

163 "Our Rules." Kickstarter. Accessed May 22, 2023. https://www.kickstarter.com/rules.

164 "Ground Rules for Hosts." Airbnb. Accessed May 22, 2023. https://www.airbnb.com/help/article/2895.

165 "Airbnb It." Airbnb. Accessed May 22, 2023. https://www.airbnb.com/host/homes?c=.pi0.pk12503328881_12472089929 1&gclid=CjwKCAjwpayjBhAnEiwA-7enawEY_ypkpwB3oo5EIkUs1K6KTQnO1mtfknmKeIkzERJb9_1GahFYy hoC2R4QAvD_BwE.

166 "Product Idea Guidelines." LEGO Ideas. Accessed May 22, 2023. https://ideas.lego.com/guidelines.

167 "Guide: Run an Employee Survey." Re:Work. Accessed July 6, 2023. https://rework.withgoogle.com/guides/analytics-run-an-employee-survey/steps/introduction/.

168 "HR Research." Amazon Jobs. Accessed July 6, 2023. https://www.amazon.jobs/en/landing_pages/hrresearch.

169 "Amazon's Tech Employees Share What It's like to Work at the Company in the Annual Tech Survey." About Amazon. October 6, 2022.

https://www.aboutamazon.com/news/workplace/new-amazon-employee-experience-survey.

170 "Shannon (Darmody) Wasiolek." Global Managing Director: Enablement, Google. Accessed November 8, 2023. https://www.linkedin.com/in/shannon-wasiolek-ab26872/.

171 "Antonio McFadden." Video + CTV Media Unification Strategy Lead - Go to Market - Americas, Google. Accessed November 8, 2023. https://www.linkedin.com/in/antonio-mcfadden-976b9421/.

172 Cox, Daniel, Juhem Navarro-Rivera, and Robert P. Jones. "Race, Religion, and Political Affiliation of Americans' Core Social Networks." PRRI. August 3, 2016. https://www.prri.org/research/poll-race-religion-politics-americans-social-networks/.

173 Ajrouch, Kristine J., Toni C. Antonucci, and Mary R. Janevic. "Social Networks Among Blacks and Whites: The Interaction Between Race and Age." *The Journals of Gerontology: Series B*, (2001). Accessed November 6, 2023. https://doi.org/10.1093/geronb/56.2.S112.

174 Adler, Lou. "New Survey Reveals 85% of All Jobs Are Filled Via Networking." LinkedIn. February 29, 2016. https://www.linkedin.com/pulse/new-survey-reveals-85-all-jobs-filled-via-networking-lou-adler/.

175 Fisher, Julia F. "How to Get a Job Often Comes Down to One Elite Personal Asset, and Many People Still Don't Realize It." CNBC. December 27, 2019. https://www.cnbc.com/2019/12/27/how-to-get-a-job-often-comes-down-to-one-elite-personal-asset.html.

176 2022. *Google Diversity Annual Report 2022*. Google Inc. https://static.googleusercontent.com/media/about.google/en//belonging/diversity-annual-report/2022/static/pdfs/google_2022_diversity_annual_report.pdf?cachebust=1093852.

177 Jones, Jeffrey M. "LGBT Identification in U.S. Ticks Up to 7.1%." Gallup. February 17, 2022. https://news.gallup.com/poll/389792/lgbt-identification-ticks-up.aspx.

178 Brown, Anna. "About 5% of Young Adults in the U.S. Say Their Gender Is Different from Their Sex Assigned at Birth." Pew Research Center. June 7, 2022. https://www.pewresearch.org/short-reads/2022/06/07/about-5-of-young-adults-in-the-u-s-say-their-gender-is-different-from-their-sex-assigned-at-birth/.

[179] Bennett, Milton J. "A Developmental Approach to Training for Intercultural Sensitivity." *International Journal of Intercultural Relations*, (1986). Accessed November 6, 2023. https://doi.org/10.1016/0147-1767(86)90005-2.

[180] Hammer, M. (2012). "The Intercultural Development Inventory: A new frontier in assessment and development of intercultural competence." In M. Vande Berg, R.M. Paige, & K.H. Lou (Eds.), Student Learning Abroad (Ch. 5, pp. 115-136). Sterling, VA: Stylus Publishing.

[181] "Intercultural Development Continuum." Intercultural Development Inventory. Accessed August 29, 2023. https://www.idiinventory.com/idc.

[182] "Learning Philosophy." Princeton University: Human Resources. Accessed November 8, 2023. https://hr.princeton.edu/learning-philosophy.

[183] Chand, Suma P., Daniel P. Kuckel, and Martin R. Huecker. "Cognitive Behavior Therapy." National Library of Medicine. May 23, 2023. https://www.ncbi.nlm.nih.gov/books/NBK470241/#:~:text=Origins%20of%20Cognitive%20Behavior%20Therapy,cognitive%20distortions%E2%80%9D%20in%20their%20thinking.

[184] Beck, Judith S., and Sarah Fleming. "A Brief History of Aaron T. Beck, MD, and Cognitive Behavior Therapy." *Clinical Psychology in Europe*, (2021). Accessed November 6, 2023. https://doi.org/10.32872/cpe.6701.

[185] "What Is Cognitive Behavior Therapy (CBT)?" Beck Institute for Cognitive Behavior Therapy. May 17, 2022. Video, https://www.youtube.com/watch?v=IlmaA5nToYM&t=168s.

[186] Duhigg, Charles. 2012. *The Power of Habit: Why We Do What We Do in Life and Business*. Random House.

[187] Fogg, BJ. 2021. *Tiny Habits: The Small Changes That Change Everything*. Harvest.

[188] Lally, Phillippa, Cornelia H. M. Van Jaarsveld, Henry W. W. Potts, and Jane Wardle. "How Are Habits Formed: Modelling Habit Formation in the Real World." *European Journal of Social Psychology*, (2009). Accessed November 6, 2023. https://doi.org/10.1002/ejsp.674.

[189] Gladwell, Malcolm. 2008. *Outliers: The Story of Success*. Little, Brown and Company.

[190] Simon, Herbert A., and William G. Chase. "Skill in Chess." *American Scientist.*, (1973). Accessed November 6, 2023.

[191] Lewin, C. G. "The Emergence of Compound Interest." *British Actuarial Journal*, (2019). Accessed November 6, 2023. https://doi.org/10.1017/S1357321719000254.

[192] "S&P 500 Historical Annual Returns." Macrotrends. Accessed July 6, 2023. https://www.macrotrends.net/2526/sp-500-historical-annual-returns.

[193] McVeigh, Kevin. "Why The S&P 500 Isn't What You Think It Is." Exchange Capital Management. September 25, 2018. https://www.exchangecapital.com/blog/why-the-sp-500-isnt-what-you-think-it-is.

[194] Knechtle, Beat, and Pantelis T. Nikolaidis. "Physiology and Pathophysiology in Ultra-Marathon Running." *Frontiers in Physiology*, (2018). Accessed November 6, 2023. https://doi.org/10.3389/fphys.2018.00634.

[195] Chan, Susie. "The Strange and Intriguing World of Running Hallucinations." *Runner's World*. February 17, 2022. https://www.runnersworld.com/uk/training/motivation/a39119399/running-hallucinations/.

[196] Wirnitzer, Katharina, Patrick Boldt, Gerold Wirnitzer, Claus Leitzmann, Derrick Tanous, Mohamad Motevalli, Thomas Rosemann, and Beat Knechtle. "Health Status of Recreational Runners over 10-km up to Ultra-marathon Distance Based on Data of the NURMI Study Step 2." *Scientific Reports*, (2022). https://doi.org/10.1038/s41598-022-13844-4.

[197] Csikszentmihalyi, Mihaly. 2008. *Flow: The Psychology of Optimal Experience*. Harper Perennial Modern Classics.

[198] "Mihaly Csikszentmihalyi: Flow, the Secret to Happiness." TED. October 24, 2008. Video, https://www.youtube.com/watch?v=fXIeFJCqsPs.

[199] "Sparrow Hospital Nurse Protects Pediatric Patient, Receives Award." Michigan Health & Hospital Association. October 21, 2021. https://www.mha.org/newsroom/sparrow-hospital-nurse-protects-pediatric-patient-receives-award/.

[200] "MIS in Children." Centers for Disease Control and Prevention. January 3, 2023. https://www.cdc.gov/mis/mis-c.html.

[201] "HGB Nurse Receives MHA Keystone Center Speak-up! Award." Sparrow. Accessed June 12, 2023. https://www.sparrow.org/news/hgb-nurse-receives-mha-keystone-center-speak-award.

[202] "War Memorial Employee Speaks Up for Patient Safety, Receives Award." Michigan Health & Hospital Association. July 21, 2021.

https://www.mha.org/newsroom/war-memorial-employee-speaks-up-for-patient-safety-receives-award/.

[203] "Bronson Battle Creek Employee Receives Award for Speaking Up for Patient's Safety." Bronson. April 6, 2021. https://www.bronsonhealth.com/news/bbc-employee-receives-mha-award-for-patient-safety/.

[204] "MHA Keystone Center Speak-up! Award." Michigan Health & Hospital Association. Accessed June 12, 2023. https://www.mha.org/about/awards/speak-up-award/#1632168099591-d19e5e25-aa20bb47-209ee37d-d7ecb403-bd87.

[205] "Jidoka – Toyota Production System Guide." *Toyota UK Magazine*. May 31, 2016. https://mag.toyota.co.uk/jidoka-toyota-production-system/.

[206] "Wrong-Site, Wrong-Procedure, and Wrong-Patient Surgery." Department of Health & Human Services: Patient Safety Network. September 7, 2019. https://psnet.ahrq.gov/primer/wrong-site-wrong-procedure-and-wrong-patient-surgery#:~:text=A%20seminal%20study%20estimated%20that,error%20every%205%E2%80%9310%20years.

[207] Tyson, Cobb K. "Wrong Site Surgery—Where Are We and What Is the Next Step?" *PubMed Central*, (2012). Accessed November 2, 2023. https://doi.org/10.1007/s11552-012-9405-5.

Made in United States
Troutdale, OR
04/02/2024